WHEN
TALK
IS NOT
CHEAP

Mandy Aftel, M.A., M FCC
& Robin Tolmach Lakoff, Ph.D.

With an Introduction by LEE COLEMAN, M.D.

WHEN TALK IS NOT CHEAP

Or, How to Find
the Right Therapist
When You Don't Know
Where to Begin

WARNER BOOKS

A Warner Communications Company

Copyright © 1985 by Mandy Aftel and Robin Tolmach Lakoff
All rights reserved.
Warner Books, Inc., 666 Fifth Avenue, New York, NY 10103

W A Warner Communications Company

Printed in the United States of America
First Printing: August 1985
10 9 8 7 6 5 4 3 2 1

Designed by Giorgetta Bell McRee

Library of Congress Cataloging in Publication Data

Aftel, Mandy.
  When talk is not cheap.

  1. Psychotherapy—Evaluation. 2. Psychotherapy.
3. Psychotherapist and patient. I. Lakoff, Robin
Tolmach. II. Title.
RC480.5.A34 1985   616.89′14   85-684
ISBN 0-446-51309-1

For Selena, Chloe, and Andy

ACKNOWLEDGMENTS

There are many people who have contributed to this book. It would be impossible to thank them all, but we would like to mention those people who have made it possible and pleasant for us.

Over the years, Mandy Aftel's clients have contributed to this project in essential ways: by allowing their sessions to be taped, so that we could analyze them; by their commitment to their therapy, and willingness to work hard and learn from it; and by what they have taught us about the process of therapy and how it works.

Our friends, too, have been a source of support and ideas. In particular we would like to thank: James C. Coyne, Diane Johnson, June McKay, Marty Olmstead, and Emmy Smith. Ann Juell and Peter Kerner, of the Educational Television Office of the University of California,

ACKNOWLEDGMENTS/viii

Berkeley, were helpful in supplying videotape equipment and personnel.

To our agent, Frederick Hill, who believed in our idea from the outset, we owe a debt of gratitude, as well as to Suzanne Lipsett, who made helpful editorial suggestions on early stages of the manuscript.

Felix qui potuit rerum cognoscere causas.

Happy is the one who understands the reasons for things.

—VERGIL

CONTENTS

WHEN TALK IS NOT CHEAP

INTRODUCTION

This is a book about shopping. Shopping for a psychotherapist. In a nation that shops as much as ours, it is remarkable that the art of selecting a therapist has received so little attention. There is, of course, a vast array of books on virtually every type of therapy available. But this book teaches that the quality of the therapist is more important than the style of therapy. "Your primary concern," the authors write, "should be the character of the therapist." This book also teaches that only the client is qualified to decide who is and who isn't a good therapist.

My own experiences as a therapist tell me how crucial are these points. The practice of psychotherapy is an art, not a science. Many therapists, however, practice what they believe is the "science" of psychiatry, or the "science" of behavior modification, and so on. These therapists are technicians, trained to treat clients with methods that are tried and true.

Other therapists, the kind this book will help you find, are artists. They are responsible and well trained, but they recognize that what they practice is not science but art. Like all artists, the quality psychotherapist knows that his or her field of expertise is too rich, too subtle, too complex to reduce to formulas. The quality psychotherapist also knows that therapy is not done to somebody but with somebody. This type of therapist is constantly striving to be a finely tuned and highly reponsive tool to be used by the client.

Too many psychotherapy clients fail to look hard enough for such a therapist. When you need a therapist, you don't feel like telling your story three or four times. You desperately want the first therapist you try to be the one for you. If doubts creep in, it is often easier to blame yourself than to question the therapist's methods.

This book is going to give you the insight and, hopefully, the courage to keep on looking until you find a therapist who is a true artist. You will recognize such a therapist most of all by one quality: his or her insistence that you are in charge. You decide which problems most need attention; you decide if the sessions are productive, and if not, why not; you decide when you've done enough and are ready to stop.

Quality therapists want it that way because they know that's the only way therapy helps. The therapeutic relationship becomes a model of power building, a microcosm that helps the client gather and use power out there in the real world. My enthusiasm for this book stems, more than anything else, from the authors' persistent reminders that the core of good therapy is a power relationship between therapist and client that puts the client in the driver's seat.

Recent trends in psychiatry make this book especially important. For the past couple of decades, the psychiatric profession has become more interested in biochemical speculations and the prescribing of pills than in the art of counseling. Thousands of patients, and their families, are being told by psychiatrists that their problems are the result not of a troubled life but of a troubled brain. The answer is Thorazine, or lithium, or Elavil. Perhaps even electroshock. Real therapy, in which the client and the therapist work together as partners, takes a back seat to the regulation of drug dosages and waiting for the pills to "work." In this kind of "therapy," the client is hardly likely to feel qualified to judge the performance of the therapist. Brain diseases and drugs are the province of doctors, not patients.

Even psychotherapists who are not psychiatrists, such as psychologists, social workers, and family counselors, are frequently hesitant to challenge psychiatry's insistence that truly serious mental disorder requires a psychiatrist who will treat the patient's "illness" with mind-altering chemicals. Persons looking for genuine psychotherapy, and not just pills, may find themselves repeatedly referred back to a psychiatrist for medications. Many therapists are too frightened to do it any other way.

This is also true of vast numbers of family physicians and general practitioners. Rather than spending time discussing emotional problems, or referring the patient for genuine therapy, the doctor gives the patient a prescription for a psychoactive medication. Along with the prescription, many patients are also given the misinformation that their type of problem is a result of faulty brain chemistry. The drug just prescribed will put things back on track again.

The troubled person looking for help thus finds, all too often, that professionals are quite adamant that only they know what is needed. Patients who have other ideas are "resistant." Their doubts are further indication of their mental illness.

Equally difficult may be the pressure coming from family members. Sometimes with the best of intentions, but sometimes for reasons of convenience or resentment, family members may insist that "the doctor knows best." Many professionals tell family members that it is their responsibility to be sure the patient stays on medications, whatever his/her wishes. When they are confronted with such professional advice, as well as the endlessly repeated (but false) claim that major mental disorders are now known to be biochemical in nature, it is little wonder that so many friends and families of mental patients have adopted such a position. What is the result? The person needing and wanting help may feel alienated from the very people who should be supportive.

Precisely because Mandy Aftel and Robin Lakoff demonstrate a deep concern for the impact of language, readers of this book will be better protected from the misunderstandings being perpetuated by the psychiatric profession. Take, for example, the woman who calls me to ask for an appointment. She tells me that during a recent hospitalization, "my psychiatrist finally discovered that I'm a manic-depressive. He says lithium will correct what's wrong in my brain, but I don't like how it makes me feel." Her mind and body tell her the lithium is not a good idea, while her psychiatrist tells her he has "diagnosed" her "illness" and "prescribed" the proper "treatment."

Only by following the approach discussed in this book will the many persons being manipulated in this way come to discover that they have not been "diagnosed," merely labeled. According to the Oxford English Dictionary, "to make a diagnosis of (a disease) [is] to distinguish and determine its nature from its symptoms." True medical diagnosis moves from symptoms to causes, and this knowledge determines the proper treatment. Despite psychiatry's rampant speculations, mental disorders have not been shown to stem from medical disorder of the brain. Even psychiatry's new diagnostic manual, "Diagnostic and Statistical Manual of Mental Disorders" (DSM III), acknowledges this when it states: "The approach taken in DSM III is atheoretical with regard to etiology. . . . "

This means that psychiatrists, and those many psychotherapists who follow their lead, are free to pick whatever label feels "best." No reliable diagnostic methods are available to settle the question definitively, as there is no known medical disorder to measure. All too often the result is that the label chosen is precisely the one that will justify a particular drug treatment. Instead of treatment evolving from legitimate diagnosis, as in medicine, the psychiatric label picked is the one the textbooks say requires a particular treatment the psychiatrist already favors. In medicine, diagnosis precedes and determines treatment, but in psychiatry, a favored treatment precedes and determines diagnosis. In medicine, diagnosis is descriptive, but in psychiatry, diagnosis is prescriptive.

Consider, for instance, a disruptive person being held on a psychiatric ward. He/she is put on Thorazine or some similar drug, and naturally the "diagnosis" is schizophrenia, because otherwise it might be recognized that the Thorazine is not treating a "disease" but merely controlling the person's behavior. If, however, the disruptive behavior continues, lithium may be added. Now the patient is a manic-depressive, as this is the "illness" said to require lithium.

The point is not that medications are never helpful but that the client—not the therapist—is the only one qualified to know if they are indeed helping. No label previously applied by a psychiatrist changes this fact. The point is also that persons wanting help for emotional problems but not wanting medications (or wanting them in lesser amounts than recommended) should be able to get help in a manner they approve. Given the current trends I have just described, and psychiatry's domination of the mental-health professions, it is clear that persons looking for help will need to adopt an attitude of independence and skepticism. The problem, of course, is that such qualities are least likely to be operating at a time when psychotherapy is felt necessary.

All the more reason, then, that this book is a valuable resource for persons seeking therapy. I hope their families and friends will read it as well, and take seriously the authors' view that "only the client can tell if the process is working as it should." To those who respond that such may be the case for "garden variety neurotics" but not for "the walking wounded," I can only echo the major themes of this book, each of which I have seen to be true in my own psychotherapy practice. First, without mutual respect between therapist and client, real therapy is impossible. Second, such respect requires a relationship in which the client, not the therapist, is ultimately in charge.

If mildly disturbed persons need this type of relationship with their therapists, more seriously disturbed persons need it even more. It is these persons, in the midst of a major depressive episode, or perhaps having slipped into a psychotic breakdown, who are least able to defend themselves against therapists who assume too much power. More seriously disturbed persons may require a kind of help different from that needed by the once-a-week office patient, but if we are to avoid frightening away the very persons who most need professional help, the vision set forth in this book should be a part of therapy with all clients.

Only therapists willing to let clients become true partners in the therapy process, and clients ready to demand such a partnership, will be able to cut through the jungle of psychiatric misinformation and manipulation that seems to be getting thicker each year. Clients will need, as the authors write, to ask, "Does [my] therapist treat [me] like a unique individual rather than a representative of a psychological 'category'?" They will need to reject the medical language of psychiatry and the chain of assumptions that is initiated by this language.

When talk is not cheap, it should at least be straight talk and not pseudomedical manipulation. This book is going to help a lot of people recognize the difference.

Lee Coleman, M.D.
Berkeley, California

Part One

GETTING INTO THERAPY

AUTHORS' INTRODUCTION

For many Americans, psychotherapy has become almost an inevitable part of life—perhaps the "pursuit of happiness" guaranteed in the Declaration of Independence. One person in four will have some personal experience with psychotherapy, but not many will receive the benefits they entered the process to achieve. For a lucky few, therapy will dramatically improve the quality of their lives: better relationships, more success at work, and a feeling of inner strength. The rest will experience a range of possibilities from disappointment to disaster: from a feeling that things haven't changed very much at the cost of a lot of money, to outright betrayal by someone who has been greatly trusted.

The problem is that buyers of therapeutic services are getting a pig in a poke: They don't know what to look for, let alone whether a particular therapist is competent. Therapists have been less than eager to police themselves, to establish standards for excellent—or even adequate—therapy and judge colleagues by them. The problem is compounded by the fact that in therapy as perhaps nowhere else, consumers have neither the education nor the self-confidence to evaluate the services they are getting. Built into therapeutic theory is the precept "The customer is always wrong." The therapist functions as the expert on the client's mind and everything that occurs during a session. So if the client feels distress over something the therapist has said, it must be the client's fault, the result of the misperceptions that brought him/her to therapy in the first place. In other fields, there is a basis for quality control. In therapy alone, malpractice is, if not encouraged, at least benignly tolerated for the simple reason that no one in a position to encounter it is considered to be in a position to criticize it.

But in fact, the way in which quality is assessed in other fields, by experts who do not themselves utilize the services, would not be effective in psychotherapy anyway: Only the client can tell if the process is working as it should. So quality control for the therapeutic profession can be achieved only by educating prospective clients and showing them what to look for and what can be accomplished, as well as what can go wrong.

In embarking on a course of therapy, perhaps more than in any other form of treatment, a new client is at a loss, not knowing what to expect. The process is mysterious; results are difficult to gauge. A book that describes the process and explains basic assumptions can do much to remove this confusion.

Many books have been written about the psychotherapeutic experience. Some, for the therapist's use, are technical: They describe the theoretical assumptions of a particular school or are concerned with the inculcation of a particular therapeutic methodology. Only a few are directed to the lay person contemplating, or engaged in, psychotherapy. Sometimes these books are aimed at debunking the value of therapy (which may be useful in offsetting some of its proponents' more exaggerated claims), but more often they attempt to be helpful to people seeking therapy. They talk about different theories, where to get referrals, the physical aspects of the therapeutic situation, etc., but they don't go into detail about how the process works or what clients can do by and for themselves to guarantee that the therapy will be fulfilling—or, to put it another way, that they will get their money's worth. While we discuss all the practical and theoretical aspects of the therapeutic experience, we are most concerned with an issue that has been given much less attention: the clients'—as well as the therapists'—responsibility in the process.

Therapy is not, in our view, something done *to* or *for* the client. It is an active process in which both participants play crucial roles. Failure to recognize and act on this may doom a client to an unsuccessful experience—or worse—even if both client and therapist start out with the best intentions in the world. So we are writing this book as a consumer's manual for prospective clients in psychotherapy, to help them learn to become sophisticated consumers who can make the most of the excellent therapist they will learn to select.

We see therapy, then, as an enterprise involving two responsible persons, not a helpless individual and a magician. This means that the client—whether before therapy begins or, more probably, as an outcome of therapy—must learn to negotiate to insure that therapy meets his/her needs, and must become aware enough of the risks entailed in the therapist's special power to neutralize some of these dangers. We consider a power imbalance between therapist and client unavoidable and essential in the therapeutic process (largely because it helps the client learn to express his/her needs) but open to misuse if the client does not remain vigilant.

In much writing about therapy, the consumer is referred to as the "patient," following the model of traditional medicine. Here we have chosen to call this person the "client," for several reasons. The doctor-patient relationship is a bad one to emulate, incorporating as it does the idea that the former alone possesses the knowledge and the authority to "cure" the illness of the latter, who must, to be "cured," remain passive, obedient, and ignorant. Nothing could be less like the image of therapy we are proposing. On the other hand, calling the consumer a "client" emphasizes the businesslike aspect of the relationship: Each participant needs the other, and each has rights. The client is paying for a service, not subjecting himself/herself to a cure. The medical model, in speaking of the patient, also suggests that the person engaging in therapy is "sick" and can be "cured." But we see the situation otherwise. The client is not sick but is experiencing difficulties; will not be "cured" but will learn new skills. The analogy, if anything, should be to education.

But even the medical patient is ahead of the therapeutic client in one respect: With the recent self-help movement and the consequent publication of many books that explain the body and its functions, demystifying the doctor's knowledge, the consumer has become both more aware of the difference between good and bad medical treatment and more demanding of the former. But psychotherapy still involves mystique: "Patients" are encouraged to "regress," to revert to a childlike state—which they are taught to believe is an essential part of the process—the deeper, the better. And children are not competent to criticize or evaluate. We do not see deep regression as an intrinsic part of therapy; good therapy can, and should, exist without this distortion. The encouragement to regress causes the consumer to spend more time and money in therapy than might otherwise be necessary—as well as increasing the therapist's relative power at the client's expense.

Bad therapy is not mere myth. We ourselves, as well as many friends and friends of friends, have dreadful stories to tell about unfortunate personal therapeutic experiences. We know now what we should have seen early on and realize that there were warning signals that should not have gone unheeded, but we didn't know what to make of them. We also know of many people who have re-entered therapy, though scarred by earlier therapeutic trauma, hoping for a more positive second chance—but having no clearer idea of what they should be looking for than they had the first time.

It is remarkable that many of these people whose experience has been negative are still believers in the process and are willing to try again. But most of us remain believers, holding on to the hope that we can make our lives better. The depiction of therapy and therapists in the media attests to that: In the last decade or so, countless books and movies have appeared with a therapist as hero or heroine, a figure almost godlike in sensitivity, wisdom, and compassion. Not surprisingly, in these works, cures are quick and permanent. We get the impression that the process is easy and relatively pleasant. These vicarious experiences have taught people to expect from a real-life therapist something that cannot be delivered and would be unsatisfactory it if were. We hope that this book will act as a corrective, a description of the actual process a prospective client can expect.

Both of the authors have been interested in the therapeutic process, and the definition of good therapy, for some time. Mandy Aftel has been in private practice as a therapist for seven years. Robin Lakoff is a professor of linguistics with interests in pragmatics and sociolinguistics—the way in which language is used in social interactions. We met in 1981, when Robin appeared at Mandy's house to buy Mandy's thirteen-volume *Oxford English Dictionary*. We gradually got to talking and discovered we shared an interest in psychotherapy. We found ourselves frequently getting together to talk, and the talk centered on certain favorite issues: how therapy worked and did not work; the power relationship between therapist and client, and the dangers therein; the ethics of therapy and the client's role in seeing that they are not violated.

Mandy described to Robin how she did therapy, and Robin was intrigued—Mandy seemed to approach therapy in a unique way. To try to isolate what made her special kind of therapy work so well, Mandy taped a series of interviews with several of her current clients (with their written permission, of course). They were striking: We began to see patterns, changes, real and dramatic *results*—through the use of techniques either unknown to, or anathema to, more orthodox therapists. We worked on the tapes, clarifying and interpreting what we heard, for two years.

As we worked and talked, we weren't sure at first where it was all leading. We considered writing, for professionals, a description of Mandy's therapeutic technique. But our hearts weren't really in it. Remembering our own experiences as clients, and the experiences our friends and Mandy's clients had told us about, we found ourselves moving more and more toward a book that would make therapy more meaningful for the client and help the client get the most out of it. We realized that what we had to say, what was profoundly important in our eyes, had to be addressed not to the therapist but to the client. We hope the book you are now holding in your hands will help to make your therapeutic experience the best it can be. Because therapy, well-conceived and well-utilized, is such a powerful tool for change and growth, perhaps the best hope for happiness, we want people to be able to derive the greatest possible benefit from it, to find the right therapist and do productive work. If, as a by-product, clients learn to demand better therapy, encourage therapists to sharpen their skills, and force the profession to better police its members, this will be a service both to future clients in therapy and to the therapeutic profession.

We have tried to write a book that is as accessible and jargon-free as possible and that encourages people to think deeply about a wide variety of relevant issues. So we have tried to avoid technical terminology insofar as possible. Where we could not, we have defined every word used in a special way in a glossary at the end of the text. The first significant occurrence in the text of an item defined in the glossary is printed in **boldface.** For readers who want to explore further the topics we discuss, there are suggested readings at the end of many chapters.

We learned a tremendous amount from writing this book; we hope you will, from reading it.

CHAPTER 1
Starting Out

You wake up in the morning and wish you hadn't. Getting out of bed is more than you can do. As the day goes on, things don't get better. Nothing you do makes you happy, but doing nothing is too depressing. Everyone you talk to gets on your nerves, but you hate the idea of being alone. At the end of the day you feel exhausted, though you haven't accomplished anything.

Anger. Confusion. Depression. These are emotions everyone feels, and people often figure out how to cope with them. But sometimes these feelings become overwhelming. The people in your life—the ones you hope will make you feel better—can't seem to make a difference, and you are beginning to feel uncomfortable bringing your problems to them. Or maybe you're not sleeping well, you're gaining

19

weight, you get one cold after another. Granted, you're having a hard time, but you should be coping with it better than this. It occurs to you that maybe you should see a psychotherapist.

But you've heard some things about therapy that make you worry. People say that in therapy you must reveal yourself totally: all those embarrassing and painful secrets you've never dared to tell anyone. Can you trust a therapist not to reject you after hearing what you have to tell? Or worse, you have a suspicion that there are some things about you so strange and terrible you can't even bear to think about them. What if they come up in therapy? Will you go completely to pieces?

There are other things you might worry about. Suppose you're a creative person—a writer, a painter, a musician. There's a theory that creativity is dependent upon neurotic suffering. What if therapy gets rid of the neurosis? Will the creativity go as well?

Or maybe you've been to a therapist before and considered it to be a waste of money. You didn't like the guy very much—he wouldn't answer your questions—and you never really felt any better, though you went for more than a year. Still, on your own you're feeling worse and worse. You muddle through somehow: You drink or take drugs, or go from partner to partner, job to job, but don't often change anything real inside. People grow older and become more bitter, placing the blame on others, but lying awake at 3:00 A.M., they come up against the nagging insight that the responsibility for their situation is their own. Could therapy, good therapy, be the answer?

Maybe you have reached this point but are afraid that finding a good therapist will be difficult, and you know that the chance of getting involved with a poor therapist isn't worth the risk. You think of a friend who seemed to have only minor problems before she started seeing a therapist. Her marriage was adequate if not all she had hoped for. When her child was four, she decided to go back to school for an advanced degree. She made satisfactory arrangements for child care and told her husband that he should start to do more of the housework than he had been used to. Very soon the marriage deteriorated into continual bickering over responsibilities. Her husband suggested that she needed therapy. Her therapist suggested that the problems in the marriage were due to the amount of time she was spending outside the home and that her husband's dissatisfaction was legitimate. She quit school and returned to being a full-time housewife, but the marriage did not improve. Now she finds it hard to get up in the morning, and household tasks don't get done.

And then there's another friend who went into therapy with a well-known and well-respected male psychotherapist. One day, when she was obviously in distress, he took her hand as she was leaving and gazed into her eyes. A few sessions later, these innocent gestures had become sex on the couch. Meanwhile, she continued paying her regular fee. Gradually she realized she was feeling no better and in fact was having more problems than ever.

Or what if therapy brings to light problems you are afraid to deal with? One man had trouble finding the "right" woman. He dated woman after woman, but as soon as there was any sign of the relationship becoming serious, he broke it off. In the course of therapy he learned a lot about himself—in particular, that he was attracted to men. This was terrifying to him. How would he tell his family? How would he deal with his male friends? He became more and more depressed. He had entered therapy hoping to resolve a relatively minor problem, but his therapy revealed something much deeper. The therapist refused to take his anxiety seriously. Because she was from a very liberal background, the idea that homosexuality could cause rejection was unthinkable to her. A more sensitive therapist could have supported him through the anguish of confronting his family.

We are writing this book to help people:

1. decide if they need therapy;
2. find the best therapist they can;
3. make their therapeutic experience as productive as possible—that is, get the most for their money;
4. guard against committing themselves to expensive but unproductive therapy.

We believe in therapy, but only when it's practiced correctly. And we believe that therapy is only practiced correctly when client and therapist both take responsibility for it. Any therapist who is uncomfortable with clients who want to take care of themselves is not a therapist for you. Beware of the therapist who expects unconditional surrender—someone who cannot hear your point of view and sees the experience as him/her leading you rather than a voyage of cooperative learning and discovery. We will help you learn what your rights are as a client and when they are being violated. But at the same time, we want to emphasize that although there are risks in therapy and caution is necessary, therapy is the best means of help when you are troubled.

Before you make a decision to look for a therapist, you may still be asking, "Is therapy really for me?" Because many people feel that therapy is a last resort for the truly desperate, they shy away from it because they consider their problems not as "desperate" as all that. Or they might believe that therapy is only for people who are weak or crazy, or who cannot function at all. Actually, the opposite is true: Individual therapy works best for people who are already functioning reasonably well. But you should not confuse functioning reasonably well with functioning as well as possible. Someone can be reasonably functional—have lasting relationships and a satisfactory job, for instance—and yet be leading a life less gratifying than possible because he/she is expending energy uselessly on compulsions, fears, or self-doubt. Anything that interferes with pleasure or competence can be an unnecessary burden. If there is a way out of it, why not try it?

It may sound as if we are suggesting that any reason you can think of to be in therapy is a good one, but this is not really the case. People go into therapy for bad as well as good reasons. A few common bad reasons are: the desire to please someone; because nobody else will listen to your problems; because everyone else is doing it.

On the other hand, there are many good reasons to go into therapy. Problems therapy can help with fall into two broadly defined categories: love and friendship, and work. Below are lists of some common problems in both categories that bring people into therapy.

LOVE AND FRIENDSHIP

1. You feel a need for intimacy but are unable to find it.
2. You're overwhelmed by loneliness.
3. You feel inferior or superior to everyone you meet.
4. You are thinking of doing something permanent (but you have persistent doubts).
   a. having an affair while married or in a marriage equivalent
   b. having a baby
   c. getting sterilized

5. Your relationships keep falling into unsatisfactory patterns.
   a. You're unable to break off unhappy relationships.
   b. You're unable to get involved in relationships.
   c. You are stuck in bad patterns as a parent.
   d. You have inappropriate emotional reactions—sometimes you are too emotional, sometimes not emotional enough; you lash out in anger, or burst into tears, without real provocation.
6. You have uncertainties about your sexual orientation.
7. Someone you love has died, and you can't get over it.

WORK

1. You can't find a job doing what you want to do.
2. You feel stuck in your work. The job you have doesn't make you feel at all happy, and you don't know what you want to do.
3. You are unable to be assertive.
4. You keep repeating unsatisfactory patterns.
   a. You're ineffective at delegating responsibility.
   b. You have perennial problems with co-workers.
   c. You are always dissatisfied with your work environment.
   d. You're unable to get things done (you have writer's block).
   e. You're ill frequently.
   f. You have difficulty finishing projects.
   g. You're constantly getting into inappropriate sexual relationships with your bosses, students, teachers.
   h. You have difficulty coping with co-workers and frequently feel victimized.

The problems we have been discussing are those that have been in your life for a long time: Rather than arising at a particular moment, with great urgency, they have been simmering on a psychic back burner as long as you can remember, maybe getting a little better or a little worse from time to time but always there—more like rheumatism than appendicitis. But people also necessarily encounter crises in their lives: sudden, unexpected, devastatingly painful events that cannot be pushed aside or minimized and that tend to be paralyzing. (When we speak of "crises," we usually mean purely negative events. But a crisis can be positive, too—say, beginning a new job you're excited about but are not sure you can handle.)

Though the pain of these is sharper, it, too, can be helped by therapy; and additionally, therapy can diminish the likelihood that certain (though by no means all) kinds of crises will occur, be repeated, or be as painful as they might otherwise be.

Below are two checklists, the first of which deals with problems of long duration, the second with "crises."

SHOULD YOU BE IN THERAPY?

Checklist 1A

ONGOING PROBLEMS CHECKLIST

	Frequently	Once in a While
1. You have trouble getting out of bed in the morning.	——	——
2. You want to sleep all the time.	——	——

	Frequently	Once in a While
3. You have been thinking about suicide.	——	——
4. Nothing seems interesting.	——	——
5. You are no longer attracted to your partner, and you don't know why.	——	——
6. Little things upset you more than they should.	——	——
7. You can't find a job doing what you want to do.	——	——
8. You keep getting into fights with friends and breaking off friendships.	——	——
9. You can't make up your mind about important things.	——	——
10. You've had a series of accidents or minor illnesses.	——	——
11. You go on buying sprees, getting things you don't need.	——	——
12. Your allergies are getting worse.	——	——
13. You can't sleep at night.	——	——
14. You're eating (drinking, smoking) more than is good for you.	——	——

	Frequently	Once in a While
15. You burst into tears without knowing why.	———	———
16. You feel you are losing control over your children.	———	———
17. You are vaguely anxious.	———	———
18. You are afraid to be alone.	———	———
19. Although you make good money, you're in debt.	———	———
20. You find it hard to make friends.	———	———

SCORING: If you have checked "once in a while" for ten or more of the above, or "frequently" for three or more, you should strongly consider therapy.

Checklist 1B

CRISIS CHECKLIST

Below are listed some debilitating crises. If you are experiencing any of these, therapy is apt to be especially helpful.

1. You are getting divorced.
2. You have lost a meaningful job.
3. Someone very important to you has died.
4. You are beginning to doubt something important you used to believe in (religion, love, ability).
5. You are pregnant, or your partner is.
6. You are beginning to doubt your sexual orientation.
7. You have sexual fantasies about your child.
8. You have suffered a debilitating accident or illness.
9. You have made a suicide attempt.

Often the first question that arises in considering therapy is, "What kind of therapy is best for me?" Books, movies, and television provide illustrations (more or less accurate) of many different kinds of therapy: psychoanalysis, **Jungian analytic psychology,** Gestalt, and others. The prospective client may assume that because these names are so prominent in discussions of therapy, the choice of method is the most important point to consider.

We believe, on the other hand, that your primary concern should be the character of the therapist. But you will still want to ask about a prospective therapist's theoretical orientation, because both the answer itself and the way in which it is given are important. Therapists often ally themselves with one school rather than another on the basis of a school's compatibility with their own personalities, so the choice of orientation is suggestive of more important considerations. Also, whether the therapist answers the question in a doctrinaire or a more open manner can be a valuable clue as to the kind of therapeutic experience you will have with him/her. Therefore, we will talk a little about the major similarities and distinctions among several of the most common forms of individual "talking" therapy. For more discussion, see the readings at the end of this chapter.

Historically, all forms of "talking" psychotherapy are derived from **psychoanalysis,** as developed by Sigmund Freud and his disciples, beginning in the last decade of the nineteenth century. More recent models diverge from psychoanalysis to a greater or lesser degree, but they all reflect that origin. Hence, they are all more alike than different, like members of a family. But as in a family, the individual differences are significant. Below, we first discuss the salient distinguishing characteristics of these models and then compare them.

1. *Duration:* The total length of time therapy usually takes, measured in months or years. Therapy may be **long-term** (more than a year) or **short-term,** one form of which is called **brief psychotherapy.**

2. *Intensity:* The number of sessions per week. **Low-intensity** therapy involves one session or fewer per week; **high-intensity,** three or more sessions per week.

3. *Mode of Communication:* The aspect of communication on which the therapy concentrates. **Verbal therapy** utilizes the client's verbal productions (words, intonation patterns, and the like) exclusively or largely, and the therapist is restricted to verbal communication alone. **Non-verbal** modes of therapy make use of the client's non-verbal behavior (*e.g.,* facial expression, gesture, posture, movements), and the client may be asked to re-enact physically what he/she is describing, to act out dreams or fantasies. The therapist may engage in physical interventions (*e.g.,* touching or massage). (Non-verbal therapy is possible only when client and therapist have access to each other's non-verbal behavior. If a therapeutic method requires the seating of the therapist out of the client's gaze, therapy will necessarily be only verbal.)

4. *Orientation:* The focus of therapeutic interest. If it is **intrapsychic,** sessions will focus on what is going on inside the client's mind: dreams, memories, anxieties, fantasies. Relationships with others will be examined largely in terms of their intrapsychic reasons and consequences. **Interpersonally** oriented therapy, on the other hand, focuses on the client's involvement in the here-and-now, on problems encountered in dealing with other people.

5. *Approach:* The therapist's role. If the therapist, as an integral part of the therapeutic process, is regularly expected to advise the client and provide suggestions about future behavior and the handling of real-life situations, the therapy is considered **directive;** otherwise, **non-directive.** (Any therapist may temporarily be directive, for instance in a severe crisis.)

A therapeutic model might theoretically combine these five aspects in all sorts of ways. Typically, though, a therapy that is of long duration will tend as well to be of high intensity, verbal, intrapsychic, and non-directive, and the converse, of course, is similarly true. It goes without saying that the longer the duration and the higher the intensity, the greater the total expense.

The adjacent chart shows how the currently most influential types of therapy are related to one another.

In general, urgent crises are best dealt with by a short-duration, interpersonal, directive approach. Once the immediate crisis is resolved, the therapy should become more intrapsychic and less directive, as the client requires less guidance and support and becomes able to focus beyond the worries of the immediate present. But a therapist who is strongly committed to only one of these approaches may find it difficult to change according to a client's needs. Such a therapist is not as good for you as one who is secure enough to borrow from each of these approaches as a client's needs dictate. These **eclectic** therapists are not always easy to find. Besides, they must be distinguished from therapists who are simply confused and have no rationale or discipline behind their experimentation.

People enter therapy at times of stress in their lives, as a last, desperate resort, invested with impossible hopes and unspeakable fears. They may imagine a therapist as a magician who can undo twenty years' worth of problems in a fifty-minute hour: The therapist says the right word, and

Model	Duration	Intensity	Mode	Orientation	Approach
psychoanalysis	long	high	verbal	intrapsychic	non-directive
psychoanalytically oriented	medium	low-medium	verbal	intrapsychic, some inter-personal	non-directive (mostly)
Jungian analytic psychology	long	low-medium	verbal	intrapsychic	non-directive
Gestalt	medium	low-medium	non-verbal	interpersonal and intra-psychic	somewhat directive
brief	short	low	verbal	interpersonal	directive

everything makes sense. This is a magical expectation, which even the best therapy cannot approximate.

Therapy is work, not magic. Further, the work is collaborative, with the client an active participant. It is a form of education, providing tools to use after the process itself is over. Just as education by itself does not make you intelligent, therapy by itself does not make you happy or "cure" you. And just as you wouldn't choose a college because the tuition is low or it's around the corner, you wouldn't choose a therapist because he/she is cheap or simply convenient. You need to know what makes therapy effective before you can make an informed choice.

Let's start with what good therapy *isn't* and what it *doesn't* do. In therapy you learn about yourself, but that knowledge doesn't give you total freedom of thought or action. It gives hope but not infinite possibility. It decreases your feeling of aloneness, but it doesn't automatically give you a circle of friends. Therapy teaches you how to understand yourself, and thereby to see at least partly why your life works the way it does, but it doesn't give you a set of infallible predictions to cover everything. It can increase your feelings of reasonable control over your environment, but it doesn't give you total or unrealistic control. Above all, the therapist doesn't make you well but only guides you to discover how to feel better.

Therapy involves growth and change, which entail pain. So if your "therapy" immediately makes you feel better, it is probably not therapeutic. Only psychotherapy—and, in our view, individual "talking" therapy of some duration—has the potential to effect change, and then only when the client is educated to participate fully. (Popular psychology books can be sources of insight and comfort; however, because they are addressed to a mass audience and are experienced passively by the reader, they are not truly therapeutic.)

Both participants must be aware that they are sharing the responsibility for the therapy. They both have jobs. The therapist's is: to listen and understand, to reflect the client's words and thoughts back to him/her, to clarify, educate, interpret. What isn't the therapist's job? To advise, seduce, be a "paid friend." The therapist's job is, in short, to enable the client to become more independent of the therapist.

The client's job is: to learn, to think and reflect, to struggle to change patterns of behavior, to develop courage, to find out about himself/herself, and to come to understand reality. What isn't the client's job? To unquestioningly accept the therapist's words, to manipulate or seduce the therapist, to be nice, adjusting—that is, to do things because doing them will create less friction.

To sum up then, suppose that before therapy, you're functioning well enough but not as well as you would like—there are difficulties, major or minor, that stand in the way of comfortable living. You're wondering as you read whether the time, trouble, risks, and expense of therapy are worth it for you: After all, you're managing well enough now. Could therapy make any real difference? What can you expect to gain from therapy?

You cannot expect a totally idyllic, stress- and crisis-free existence. Some stress inevitably comes from external circumstances, and even the best therapy will not make you immune to the demands of your own psyche. Life will still have downs to punctuate the ups.

You *can* expect, though, to recover more quickly and completely from painful experiences. You will feel competent because the recovery comes through your own skills and understanding. You'll feel more in control. It's like taking a course in auto mechanics. Your car may still break down, but you'll be able to tell how serious the problem is, when to get something fixed, and when to ignore it, and often you'll be able to fix it yourself.

Also, because you will have become more comfortable about yourself and your feelings and needs, you will find it easier to enjoy life, and you'll feel less guilty about experiencing pleasure. You will be less anxious and fearful. You might therefore find it easier to be open and accepting of yourself and others, so that friendship and intimacy will be less difficult.

If you have felt indecisive and unable to make commitments in the past, that might be because you are afraid of the risk commitment entails. Once you can overcome that, you will find it less troublesome to decide what you want to do in life—and with whom.

The list could go on at length, varying according to the particular difficulties you have at the start. The point is, though, that good therapy helps a person who is already functioning "well enough" to function better. You are wasting energy and time enjoying and accomplishing less than you could. Why not see how much is possible?

SUGGESTED READING

Kovel, Joel, *A Complete Guide to Therapy: From Psychotherapy to Behavior Modification*. New York, Pantheon, 1977.

Storr, Anthony, *The Art of Psychotherapy*. New York, Methuen, 1979.

Weinberg, George, *The Heart of Psychotherapy*. New York, St. Martin's Press, 1984.

CHAPTER 2

What Kind of Therapy for You?

Now you know something about what therapy can do and some basic characteristics of the most popular therapies. But you still don't have a very clear idea of what will *happen* to you once you are in therapy: what it will feel like, how you will be helped to change. While you may be familiar with the names of different systems, you don't really know which one is best suited to your own character and problems.

You may have the idea that the choice of therapy is the most important decision you have to make. But as we have said, we feel that the personality and skill of the individual therapist are much more important for a successful outcome than the particular system that a therapist practices. Therapy is a combination of art and science. The science is the system itself, its rules and assumptions. But the art is in the practitioner's intuition, sensitivity, and intelligence, as well as his/her ability to work well with a particular client. In a later chapter we will talk about how to assess a therapist's skills. But it will be useful for us now to see what the theory a therapist believes in contributes to the experience of being in therapy.

The experience of therapy depends on many factors. First, there is what you bring to the process: your hopes and fears about therapy and about yourself, and your prior experience in life, as well as what you hope to accomplish. Then there is the therapist: his/her rapport with you, personality, and insightfulness, combined with a possible resemblance to significant people in your past. Finally, it is important that the therapeutic model that is chosen be one that is comfortable, given your own personality and needs.

Before you begin to interview therapists, you should have some idea of what your ideal therapeutic experience would be. You should also consider your absolute "bottom line"— the basic requirements without which therapy would not be successful for you. While you'll be hoping for the ideal, awareness of your "bottom line" cutoff may keep you from entering a therapeutic relationship that is bound to fail. Checklist 2 suggests some questions you can ask yourself.

Checklist 2

YOUR REQUIREMENTS IN THERAPY

1. Should therapy be long- or short-term? Take into consideration both the speed with which you want to proceed and the urgency of your problems, as well as your willingness and ability to expend quantities of time and money.

2. How deep do you want to go? Will you be content to solve a current problem without exploring its causes or connections with other things in your life? Or do you want to use therapy as a way of gaining self-knowledge?
3. Are you more comfortable expressing things verbally or through symbolic physical action? And if you are more comfortable with one, should the therapy you choose utilize this method or the other? In other words, will your therapeutic experience be more meaningful if you go against the grain, learning to communicate in a new way, or will you achieve results faster by using the skills you possess already?
4. Is your problem one best dealt with by yourself, or does it crucially involve people close to you? In the latter case, do you want to work specifically on the way you interact with people, or would you rather understand these difficulties as stemming from your own internal needs and desires?
5. Do you want a therapeutic situation in which you can count on the therapist to tell you what to think about and talk about, and to provide guidance in your life? Or would you rather take the initiative and select your own topics?

Use your answers to narrow down your choices, basing your conclusions on the discussion in the remainder of this chapter. For example, if you are interested in long-term therapy, you might want to choose a psychoanalytically oriented model. But if it is important to you to solve a problem quickly, or if time and money are significant considerations despite the prestige and glamour attached to psychoanalysis, it is probably not the best therapy for you. While our discussion is obviously not exhaustive (there are currently scores of systems and sub-systems, as well as an infinity of possible and actual combinations), the currently popular therapies we discuss below have been chosen because they are probably the most distinctive forms, as well as perhaps the most common.

Our discussion, however, will not include a therapeutic model we assessed favorably in the last chapter, eclectic therapy, as it is an amalgam of the best of several approaches and so cannot be set in contrast to the others.

PSYCHOANALYSIS AND PSYCHOANALYTICALLY ORIENTED THERAPY

For many people, psychoanalysis is virtually synonymous with psychotherapy; for others, it is the most glamorous and "legitimate" model. But although psychoanalysis has prestige because it was the first form of therapy from which most others are derived, it is not necessarily the best for everyone. (Most eclectic therapists are trained in psychoanalytic theory but are able to borrow from other techniques to make their work more effective.) Very closely related is **psychoanalytically oriented psychotherapy,** which utilizes most of the assumptions of psychoanalysis but has adapted its technique to fit modern needs: shorter duration, fewer sessions per week, less emphasis on the unconscious.

What is a typical analytic hour like? You may be familiar with it through movies and books: The patient (as the client is called in analysis) lies on a couch, unable to see the analyst; the latter has only a partial view of the patient (in other words, no eye contact), being seated behind the patient's head. Much discussion of analytic technique is framed in negatives: The analyst scarcely speaks, allows a minimum of his/her personality to be perceptible, is a passive listener rather than an active participant. The analyst's traditional role is only to make interpretations, relating the patient's reports to unconscious processes. The atmosphere is often cold and distant: Analytic theory assumes that any warmth or emotional rapport provides "gratification" that militates against the patient's willingness to do the hard analytic work. Analysts tend to charge higher rates per hour than other therapists, and true analysis requires a minimum of three hours per week for several years. (Of course, many analysts, starting with Freud himself, have modified the austerity of the analytic situation, and today analysts tend to be more active than in the past. Still, "neutrality" remains an ideal that will color the experience.)

A problem with analysis is that because of its focus on the past, it may discourage the patient from making needed changes in life: The process subordinates action to reflection. Similarly, the analytic relationship tends to become one of dependency that discourages independent action and encourages interminable analysis. The stories you may have heard about people who have been in analysis for decades are not mere myths.

Because of its emphasis on the past and the unconscious, psychoanalysis is not oriented toward severe or urgent current problems or those that impair articulate communication or the development of insight, such as psychoses and addictions. It can work effectively for sexual problems and problems in relationships—in particular, problems that originate unilaterally within oneself rather than in the relationship between individuals. Analysis is best for people whose lives are generally under control: people with good verbal capacity, settled lives, and the ability to form relationships of some depth and to tolerate frustration.

Much of what has been said about psychoanalysis proper

can be said of psychoanalytically oriented therapy. Here, too, the emphasis on the unconscious and the past tends to delay the finding of solutions and discourage the growth of autonomy. There does tend to be a warmer and more "real" relationship with the therapist, who tends to participate more directly, making the discourse more like a two-person conversation and less of a monologue.

The picture we have presented of psychoanalysis may be overly negative and may fail to explain why analysis has made advocates of so many former patients. The excitement of self-discovery—deeper in analysis than in most other approaches—coupled with the emotional pleasure of working together with someone in a therapeutic relationship that develops significantly over time makes the experience worthwhile for many people.

GESTALT THERAPY

Gestalt is in many ways the reverse of analysis. Where analysis concentrates on the past from an intellectual perspective, Gestalt focuses on the client's here-and-now emotional responses to present situations. Instead of interpretation, it uses direct confrontation. Where an analyst, listening to a patient's monologue, might say, "It sounds as if you're angry at your mother," the Gestalt therapist would say, "Here's a pillow. Pretend it's your mother and express what you're feeling right now toward her."

The client talks a lot, for the purpose of expressing feelings, not for intellectual self-knowledge, which is viewed by Gestalt practitioners as a way of avoiding one's real feelings. Dramatization, as in the example above, is important. The Gestalt therapist encourages the client to act out conflicts or dreams as a way of *expressing*, rather than analyzing, feelings. For example, a client can be asked to sit in either of two chairs alternately, taking the roles of two participants in a conflict.

The duration of Gestalt therapy is normally not as long as analysis, nor are sessions usually more frequent than once a week (sometimes therapy is done in intensive, weekend-long workshops). Emotionally it can be more intense and draining than analysis. Since Gestalt therapists tend to be not soothing or reassuring but confrontational, it is not a good choice for anyone who is already in psychological crisis and in need of support. Gestalt does not focus on the rational part of the mind or on the past. Hence it might be better than an analytic approach for a highly intellectual person whose relationships are stiff and wooden or for someone who tends toward obsessional thinking. It is a way to compel someone to confront feelings, even someone who habitually is shielded from them.

BEHAVIOR MODIFICATION

The therapeutic systems we have described above are similar in that they achieve results through the client's talking about his/her problems and the therapist's making a verbal response. Behavior modification is different, because talking is limited to a discussion of the symptoms themselves and what action the therapist proposes to lessen them. In the other therapies we have mentioned, talk largely replaces direct action in the real world; even the symbolic actions of Gestalt therapy are more in the interest of communication than of effecting direct change in the client's behavior. In behavior modification, the symptom is targeted as the focus of action, usually distressing behavior in the client that can be pinpointed, such as a debilitating fear (*e.g.*, fear of flying or of leaving the house) or a destructive habit (smoking, drug addiction, or the inability to be assertive). Therefore, this kind of therapy is not well-suited to diffuse discomforts: problems in relationships or at work, for instance.

Behavior modification therapy is normally of low intensity (not more than once a week) and of short duration (no more than a few months). Client and therapist agree in advance about what the goals of the therapy are. Everything but the particular problem the client wants to solve is outside the scope of discussion. Because of its inherent limitations, behavior modification is significantly less expensive than other therapies.

The method by which behavior modification works on symptoms is called *desensitization*. The therapist starts by helping the client to relax through suggestion and guided fantasy. Suppose a client wants to get over a fear of airplane travel. The therapist might first take the client to the airport. They do nothing more than merely sit in the airport lounge watching the planes take off. The client might feel mild anxiety but nothing like the terror of actually being on a plane in the air. The next week, the therapist might have the client sit in a stationary plane. Again, the level of anxiety is manageable. Feeling anxiety dissipate in a situation that was formerly terrifying gives the client a sense of optimism and competence, which in turn makes the client more capable of overcoming the fear. Eventually, by slow degrees, the client finds himself/herself in a plane that is actually aloft, and without too much anxiety. In this way, an overwhelming, unmanageable fear can be brought under control, once it is broken down into a collection of smaller, discrete fears that can be dispelled one by one.

While behavior modification avoids some of the dangers of other therapies, such as the tendency toward inaction and overdependence on the therapist, it has risks of its own: the therapist's manipulativeness and total emphasis on objective external behavior. In this kind of therapy the client tends to be a pawn rather than a human being with an inner life.

NON-INDIVIDUAL THERAPIES

In the sections above, as elsewhere in this book, we have looked at therapy as an individual process done by a single client in partnership with a therapist. But in most types of therapy, there is the alternative of seeing a therapist as a member of a group or with other members of one's family or an important partner. In each of these alternatives, the theoretical assumptions remain the same, but the method may change and the client's experience will be rather different than in individual therapy.

In non-individual therapies, the emphasis shifts from concern for the individual's internal states to interest in his/her difficulties in interacting with others—in general, as in group therapy or with significant others in family or couple therapy. Being in therapy of this type tends to encourage group members to experiment in relationships, at first within the therapy itself, and later, ideally, in real relationships: to run risks, to make changes.

Group therapy has the advantages of generally being less expensive than individual therapy of the same type, being of shorter duration, and involving less dependence on the therapist. In group therapy, clients learn to see themselves as others see them. The experience therefore tends to be intense, with dramatic revelations. Change occurs through corrective emotional experiences that happen in group sessions: An individual's action is perceived and confronted by the other members of the group immediately as it occurs rather than (as in individual therapy) being reflected upon later, in safety.

Group therapy tends to deal with the group's dynamics rather than with each member's individual needs, which may make for less effective therapy. The qualities of the other members of the group, along with the therapist's effectiveness, determine to a considerable extent what the results of the experience will be. Particularly dangerous might be a group with a few insensitive or sadistic members and a leader who is unwilling to intervene to protect weaker members from aggression.

Therefore it is important to consider the personality of the group leader. A passive leader might create an unproductive and unfocused group; a confronting and self-important leader could encourage tyrannical tendencies in the group. So the personality of the leader outweighs his/ her theoretical orientation (as always).

Couple and family therapy most often take the form of brief therapy, which utilizes a limited number of sessions to resolve a problem. This limitation tends to reduce the development of dependency on the therapist and to focus clients' attention on their interactions with one another. Here, too, emphasis is on interactive processes, to see and change those that are unsatisfactory, rather than on the understanding of deep-seated individual reasons for them. Interpretation is discouraged. All members of the family or both members of the couple are typically seen together, sometimes by one therapist, sometimes by two co-therapists (the therapists may "model" desirable forms of interaction in contrast with what clients are actually doing). Change is encouraged by the use of assigned homework, in which clients are instructed to deliberately change some aspect of their interaction and observe the results.

These forms of therapy are less expensive than individual therapy and are particularly able to illuminate some kinds of problems. If each member of a couple in trouble enters individual therapy, there is a better-than-average chance that the relationship will break up as both become involved in their own separate needs, but if they are seen as a couple, there is a greater chance of their staying together.

Family therapy is particularly useful when the *family* as a unit is troubled, and especially when the severe problems of one member are traceable to the interactional patterns of the family unit itself: if, for example, a child is schizophrenic or anorexic. Family therapy can also be particularly helpful to a child as an alternative to individual therapy, in which he/she may come to feel like the "sick one" or the one who is at fault; in family therapy, it becomes clear what the parents' involvement is, and the child bears less of the onus.

In family or couple therapy, the potential for exacerbating pre-existing conflict is great and dangerous; a therapist who does not have an optimistic and positive outlook can make a difficult situation even worse. Also, a therapist who openly forms alliances with the more powerful member or members of the family or couple and thereby strengthens the status quo can do damage to the weaker members.

The reader may be left with a sense of uncertainty: How much better is one form of therapy than another? Are there any scientific results that bear on this crucial question? Indeed, over the years a great many attempts have been made to rate, more or less quantitatively, one therapy against another. Overall, the conclusion seems to be this: Therapy is better than no therapy (although there is some evidence that the *desire* to be in therapy is almost as helpful as the actual experience), but no system is better than any other. This conclusion holds even (in most cases) when comparing therapies in terms of the relief of specific symptoms, although behavior modification does appear to have an edge over the others in dealing with phobias and habits. Yet we know that some people get more out of their therapy than others. All that can be concluded from this is what has already been emphasized: It is the ability and personality of the therapist, rather than his/her particular theory, that determine the worth of therapy.

CHAPTER 3

Finding a Therapist

A fter reading the last chapter, you may be convinced that you would profit from therapy. But you may be uncertain about how to proceed. You're aware that good therapy could be very helpful. But bad therapy could be disastrous. How do you find a good therapist? You need leads in order to find a therapist, as you do with other kinds of help—a plumber, hairdresser, or doctor.

Therapists, like other professionals, are listed in the Yellow Pages of the telephone directory, under the following headings: Marriage and Family Counselors, Social Workers, and Psychologists. Psychiatrists are listed under Physicians. If you have no other sources, you can start here, in alphabetical order or according to geographical proximity. Calling someone listed here is the chanciest approach, but it can be used in conjunction with other methods we will describe. This chapter will help you determine, on the basis of one or two interviews, the quality of the treatment a prospective therapist can provide.

You should be prepared to spend between $100 and $200 on these preliminary interviews. This may seem like a lot of money thrown away, but you should think of it as part of the price of good therapy.

Because people think of therapists as being, like doctors, members of helping professions, they often turn to their family doctor for a **referral.** This can be a helpful place to start, but there are some things to keep in mind. Your family doctor knows your body better than your mind and therefore may not know which therapist you could work best with. Besides, your family doctor may not know very much about psychotherapy. And finally, being a physician, your doctor is apt to refer you to another medical doctor such as a psychiatrist, without considering other options. If you do get a referral from your family doctor, be especially vigilant in your interviewing of the therapist: Don't assume your doctor has done the work for you.

You may have met socially a therapist whom you would like to interview. Most therapists are reluctant to take into treatment people with whom they have a social relationship. In this case, you might want to ask him/her for a referral to another therapist. But if you have just met, acquaintanceship will probably not be a problem. Although a referral from one therapist is a good way to find another, you should remember that therapists know one another only as colleagues and have no experience of what it is like to be a particular therapist's client. The way therapists talk to one another about their clients reflects only one view of the therapeutic interaction; perhaps the client sees things in another, markedly different manner.

Perhaps you have a friend who is enthusiastic about his/ her therapist and who seems to you really to have changed for the better while in therapy. Accept the referral, but remember that a therapist who works well with one person may be less effective with another. A friend, however, knows a lot about you, and someone who has worked with a therapist usually has some sense of the therapist's personality and skill. This is the best source for a referral.

Seeing a therapist recommended by a friend may seem an ideal solution to you. At the beginning of your search, any therapist is an unknown quantity, a stranger. But if you decide to see your friend's therapist, much of the uncertainty is removed. The therapist, while not quite someone you know, isn't a complete stranger either. Besides, choosing a friend's therapist is a compliment to the friend and will make both of you feel good about each other. Nonetheless, you should enter into this situation only after careful thought, as it is fraught with potential problems. **Confidentiality,** competition, and possessiveness create difficulties for people in a close relationship who are seeing the same therapist. After entrusting your therapist with a confidence about your friend, especially one that is negative, you may be afraid that the therapist will reject one or both of you, or that, inadvertently or otherwise, the therapist will betray your confidence to your friend. A good therapist will never intentionally do either, but accidents happen to the best of us, and your fear that it *might* happen could be a hindrance to the full disclosure essential in therapy, or at least could exacerbate the anxiety that is always a part of the process.

Another problem arises out of a typical fantasy: being the therapist's favorite (or only) client. Because sharing a therapist with a friend conflicts with this fantasy, you may find yourself feeling competitive and jealous. (You may want to bear this in mind if you are ever tempted to give a friend your therapist's name.) A skillful therapist can help you work this out and utilize it in the therapeutic process. But it may be more comfortable for you not to share your therapist with your friends.

Once you have found the names of two or three therapists by using one or more of these methods, phone each of them to make an appointment. On the telephone, after telling the therapist how you got his/her name, say that you would like to make an appointment. Don't try to interview the therapist on the telephone. To a therapist, time is money, and you are wasting time. The therapist may seem brusque or cold, which may not reflect his/her true character. Talking to strangers on the phone, people often project inaccurate versions of their personalities, seeming colder or more distant than they really are in person. Even though this initial phone contact may raise questions or create anxieties, you should wait until you are face to face with the therapist before you ask for answers or reassurance.

You have located a therapist and made an appointment. Now maybe you feel scared as you enter the office. What are you going to say? Will the therapist like you—or accept you as a client? Will the therapist think you're smart or interesting enough? Can you fill up the hour with what you have to say, or will you fall silent halfway through? Will the therapist make you lie on the couch, and will that feel weird? What if the therapist reminds you of your mother? These worries are normal, but try to overcome them for now; your task in this first hour is to evaluate the therapist, not to prove yourself as a potential client.

Most likely, the first thing the therapist will say is, "What brought you here?" or "Why do you want to enter therapy?" Sometimes it's hard to give a specific reason; all you can think of is that life is overwhelming you. You can start in with just those words if you like—the therapist will probably help you focus on details. Or you might think back to your answers to the checklists in Chapter 1 and use these as the basis for your response to the therapist's question. Especially if you find the going difficult at first, the therapist should help you along—by asking questions and perhaps supplying occasional words as well as by indicating understanding (or uncertainty), verbally or otherwise. The therapist who, by silence or unresponsiveness, makes you feel more anxious, stupid, or hostile is not the therapist you should select. As you're talking, you should bear in mind that this interview is occurring on two levels for both of you. The therapist is listening to the content of what you're saying, getting a rough idea of how you see your problems, and on another level, taking in non-verbal cues: the way you sit, whether you make eye contact, whether there is a match between what you say and how you say it. By this means, the therapist is trying to determine how successfully he/she can work with you. The therapist won't be making this decision on the basis of your cleverness or articulateness but rather on the match between your personality and his/hers, and the likelihood of his/her being able to help you. On your part, you are listening to what the therapist says in response to you, the rules he/she states and the way they are stated; you are being careful to notice the therapist's non-verbal behavior (*e.g.*, smiling and eye contact) and the clarity and candor of the therapist's answers to your questions. On another level, you are determining how it *feels* to be with this therapist: Do you feel understood, liked, and respected? You may find revealing yourself difficult and may worry about whether this means therapy isn't possible for you. As long as the therapist is reasonably encouraging, don't take this problem too seriously now; it is normal to feel awkward opening up to a stranger.

The therapist should be clear at the first interview about the rules that will govern the therapeutic interaction. Ideally the therapist will broach the matter spontaneously; otherwise, you'll have to do so and note his/her response. What is the therapist's policy on cancellations? Some therapists require that you cancel twenty-four hours in advance in order not to be charged for the hour. Other therapists hold you responsible for your appointment time, and even if you cancel in advance you are still responsible for payment. A therapist's rules about this are important to know at the outset. You should ask about other matters of policy: Can you get extra appointments when you need them? What happens if you are late for the hour? What if the therapist is late? How long is the hour—forty-five or fifty minutes? What about payment: Should you pay at each session? Will it be covered by insurance? If so, will you or your insurance company be billed? If the bill is given to you monthly, what is the due date for payment?

Some therapists use written contracts to cover the issues above. Written contracts can be checked when disputes arise and can give both participants a feeling of security, but they may make negotiation difficult or impossible—and negotiation is one of the skills you should learn from the process of therapy. Having no formal contract feels friendlier and more spontaneous, besides allowing for changes by mutual agreement. But there can be misunderstandings, and the stronger party (the therapist) can take advantage of lapses of memory or points that were not made clear at the outset. In any case, you should try to be as precise as possible about the rules from the start. Although insisting on clarification may be difficult, you should not be willing to work with a therapist who:

1. refuses to talk about rules at all;
2. refuses to clarify or justify the rules;
3. refuses to consider changes that are important to you.

Checklist 3A suggests questions that you should ask during your first interview about the therapist's ways of doing therapy, basic rules, and assumptions. If you're afraid you won't remember the questions at the interview, bring the checklist along with you.

Checklist 3A

WHAT TO ASK THE THERAPIST

1. How long is a therapy session?
2. Can I get extra appointments if I need them?
3. How often should I see you?
4. What happens if I'm late for a session? What if you're late?
5. If I need to cancel a session, will I be charged for it?
6. How much do you charge?
7. Do you accept insurance?
8. What is your theoretical orientation?
9. How long do you think I'll need to be in therapy?
10. Have you been in therapy yourself? What did you get out of it?

SCORING: Questions 1 through 7 are simple and direct, and require only a short answer from the therapist. They concern the ground rules under which the therapy takes place. You should expect the therapist to answer you clearly and respectfully. Questions 8 through 10 are more complicated. You are asking them less to get the actual information than to gauge the therapist's response. The therapist should not be defensive or, in response to question 9, be afraid to say, "I don't know." In response to question 8, the therapist might name a school of therapy or might say that he/she takes an eclectic approach. You shouldn't expect a detailed answer to question 10 but only a sincere and open reply.

Sometimes a client feels that a therapist of one sex rather than the other would be more appropriate for the work that needs to be done. Or you may just have a "gut" feeling that seeing a man—or a woman—would be more comfortable. In either case, you should consider these feelings carefully but guard against taking them at face value.

For the female client, the decision is especially complicated. In everyday life, women frequently feel powerless in relation to men, or at least subordinate to them. Because power is a crucial issue in therapy (a topic we will discuss later), women need to be wary of entering a relationship in which the imbalance of power in favor of the therapist is combined with the imbalance of power in favor of men: The combination of the therapist's special power and masculine special power can be misused, with a potential for devastating damage to a female client. A woman therefore should be very careful of a prospective male therapist's attitudes as well as her own reactions to him. She should feel he respects her fully and treats her neither as a potential sexual partner nor as daddy's little girl. You may feel that because the therapist knows so much more than you, and you are coming to him for help, you are not entitled to his respect. This is an incorrect assumption. During the course of your therapy, you should be alert to subtle cues that indicate sexism: for instance, the therapist's undermining your ambition or criticizing it, consistently resolving marital disputes in favor of your husband, talking about other women in a condescending way, or telling jokes that reflect poorly on women. If you see evidence of such attitudes, you should ask point-blank about them: "Do you think a woman should stay home with her children?" "Do you think a woman should subordinate her career to that of her husband?" "Am I wrong to want to give custody of our child to my ex-husband?" Watch not only for the content of answers but for any evidence that the therapist is not taking your questions seriously, is patronizing you, or is uncomfortable with the nature of the discussion.

Sometimes women believe that any female therapist is a feminist therapist. This is not necessarily so. If a feminist orientation is important to you, you will have to question the therapist closely to discover her attitudes.

Men should also inspect their attitudes, as well as the therapist's, about gender roles. A man may hope that a woman will be easier to manipulate or control than a man, or he may be looking for someone to mother him. He should be wary of a woman therapist who seems to want to be a mother to him: for instance, someone who is critical of his girl friends or overly solicitous of his needs.

Both men and women should be wary of selecting a therapist, of either gender, who seems too "nice": too tolerant, too unwilling or unable to point out difficult things to you or insist that you focus on them. Good therapy is tough, and a therapist, to be effective, must be able to be severe with you when necessary.

At this point, you have interviewed two or three therapists. (You should interview at least two and no more than three.) You have seen each therapist no more than twice. (If you find it hard to choose at this point, the reason is probably not that you don't have enough information yet but rather that you are delaying the decision as a way of avoiding starting therapy.) Now is the time to choose one of the therapists. Maybe it is clear to you which you want to work with. But there's still a problem: How do you say no to the other(s)?

First of all, you don't have to say "no" face to face—you can use the telephone. There is no need to explain or apologize. Don't worry about hurting the therapist's feelings. You can say something like, "I have decided to work with someone else. Thank you for your time." Call the therapist you have chosen and make an appointment.

To help you reach a decision, Checklist 3B provides some questions to ask yourself after each interview, to see if the therapist is one you can work well with. Many of the questions will have to be answered impressionistically, but it's perfectly reasonable to go with your intuitions in selecting a therapist.

Checklist 3B

Therapist Evaluation

HOW TO TELL IF YOU HAVE FOUND SOMEONE YOU CAN WORK WITH

Name of therapist:
Address:
Phone number:
Date of visit:

	Yes	No	Comments
1. Did the therapist seem to understand what you were trying to say?	___	___	___
2. Was the therapist someone you could learn to trust?	___	___	___

	Yes	No	Comments

3. Were you able to clarify your position when you felt misunderstood?

4. Were you able to be honest and direct?

5. Did the therapist maintain eye contact with you?

6. Did you feel the therapist was interested in you (not preoccupied with other things)?

7. If the phone rang, did the therapist handle the interruption in a way that did not interfere with your session?

8. Did the therapist give you adequate feedback?

9. Did the therapist make a direct statement about wanting to work with you?

10. Could you and the therapist decide on a fee that was comfortable for both of you?

11. Did the therapist seem flexible?

12. Did the therapist make the rules clear at the outset?

	Yes	No	Comments
13. Could you ask for explanations when the therapist suggested rules the reasons for which you did not understand?	———	———	———

SCORING: For questions 1, 2, 5, 6, 11, 12, and 13, count two points for each "yes" answer. For the other questions, count one point for each "yes." Score as follows:

15–20 points: a good choice
10–15 points: questionable
under 10 points: a poor choice

CHAPTER 4

Special Consumers of Therapy

People think about entering therapy for different reasons and require different things from their therapists. Before you find yourself firmly committed to a particular therapist, you should consider any special needs or requirements you have, and on this basis, determine whether you can get what you need from your therapeutic experience.

Historically, psychotherapy was developed, beginning about the turn of the century, to answer the needs of a specific group, identified in terms of their socioeconomic and educational status. Most of these early participants were white, middle-to-upper class, and well-educated. This remains the case today, and additionally, therapists themselves tend to come from this group. Because people most readily understand and sympathize with ways of talking and living similar to their own, and because the forms themselves that therapy takes were devised to be most comfortable to people in the above group, therapy remains most readily accessible to people in that group.

Additionally, and perhaps more significantly, therapists tend to feel most comfortable working with members of certain psychologically (as opposed to socially) defined groups. This phenomenon is so generally acknowledged that one group has (only partly tongue in cheek) been given a name, **YAVIS,** an acronym standing for Young, Attractive, Verbal, Intelligent, and Successful. These people are more appealing than others to many therapists, and as a consequence, they are more often given encouragement to enter therapy, and remain in it longer, than members of other groups—and, incidentally, probably have pleasanter experiences in therapy.

This is not to say, of course, that only members of the group mentioned above should be in therapy or can profit from therapy. But it does mean that others must approach the problems of finding a therapist and making the therapeutic experience maximally useful with especial caution, and they should be prepared to do more work themselves to insure success. In addition, they should steel themselves for some more or less negative experiences that members of favored groups are less likely to encounter. Should these experiences occur, they should realize that it is not *they* who are to blame but the prejudices and preconceptions of the therapeutic establishment. People over fifty and members of minorities are examples.

There are other groups, too, whose members are particularly at risk in one way or another. Some face a conflict between their own personal needs for autonomy (which therapy should encourage) and the stereotypes of society, which therapists often unquestioningly adopt, about how members of such groups, to be "healthy," ought to "adjust" to meet the needs and expectations of society as a whole—the opposite of autonomy. It is particularly important for members of such groups who enter therapy to select therapists who will work for *them*, not for their families or society. Women and gay people are examples.

Then there are people whose experience in therapy is made more complex for unavoidable economic, as well as emotional, reasons. In general, the therapeutic relationship is, and ought to be, a dyad: a dialogue between two people, therapist and client, and involving only these two. If this is the case, the client is responsible for making the arrangements to enter therapy, keeping appointments, paying bills, and deciding how long to keep going. Under these conditions, the therapist is likely to be responsive to the client's needs.

But some clients are financially (and often emotionally) dependent on someone else. Adolescents are one example; sometimes married women with no independent income fall into this category. When one person determines that another should (or should not) be in therapy, or stay in therapy, or see a particular kind of therapist, the **dependent person**'s options are lessened, and with them the chances of developing autonomy. More dangerously, it too often happens that a therapist who is seeing a client whose bills are being paid by another person becomes confused about whom he/she is working for. Correctly, the therapist is working only for the client, in the client's interests, but if the client and the bill-payer have different ideas about what the client needs or wants, whose side is the therapist to take? The temptation is often to side with the person who is paying the bills (who is usually more powerful and influential socially, and thus more persuasive) and thus to see the job of therapy as making the client a better child, or wife, for someone else, rather than a more autonomous human being.

Still others are at risk because the pattern of their lives is—by choice or necessity—threateningly different from that of most people. A therapist may see it as the task of therapy to make these people behave more in accordance with what society sees as "right" or "normal" rather than helping them to lead their lives in the happiest and most productive way for *them*. Artists are one such group.

Finally, there are clients who cannot choose therapy, or a therapist, for themselves; others must make the determination. These are children, whose parents must make decisions for them with special wisdom and courage.

Although these groups have some special needs, in most respects they are like other therapeutic consumers and can use the bulk of this book like other readers. Their main concerns center on a therapist's possible incorrect preconceptions of them as members of special groups. The groups we will be discussing are: (1) artists; (2) dependent people; (3) minorities; (4) gay people; (5) people over fifty; (6) women.

ARTISTS

(We will use the term **artist** to refer to a range of people engaged in creative activity: painters, writers, sculptors, performers, and others.) While artists come to therapy with many of the same problems faced by everyone else, the special conditions their work places on their lives require unusual empathy and understanding from a therapist. Artists usually work alone and either get no criticism or attention from anyone or too much of a negative kind. They tend to lead rather isolated lives—working at odd hours, locking themselves away from human companionship for long periods of intense activity, then apparently doing nothing for long stretches while the rest of the world works regular nine-to-five days. This sort of pattern puts strains on relationships and can cause artists depression and confusion. In other kinds of work, there are usually supervisors to inspire productivity, but artists work under pressure only from themselves.

Then, too, virtually all artists will at some time suffer from an inability to work. They feel "blocked," although they desperately want to be productive. The longer they go on without working, the more anxious they become. The greater their anxiety, the less is their ability to work. They— and the outside world—see their predicament as unrelated to the anxieties others face in their work and therefore as something too mysterious to be understood by anyone else, including the therapist. In fact, this is how people tend to view creative work in general: as a mysterious activity unlike ordinary psychological processes, too delicate to be examined and akin to magic. Very often, for this reason, artists are reluctant to enter therapy and expose their creativity to scrutiny, for fear it will disappear if looked at. And even when artists are involved in therapy, they may feel reluctant to examine their work, or even their way of working.

Creative work has symbolic meaning for those who do it. Work can resolve psychological conflicts and bring deep satisfaction. But the symbolic power of creative work has its dangers, not unlike those of therapy: the revelation of fears, wishes, and secrets can cause guilt and anxiety, which in turn make work more difficult. Therapy can be especially useful to someone caught in this kind of conflict. The therapist's encouragement and support can extend into the creative work, giving the artist strength enough to bring painful feelings to full consciousness, perhaps to be incorporated later into the work of art. Writing, in particular (like therapy), by forcing one to put frightening feelings into concrete words, can lessen the force of inner conflicts.

Artistic work is also like therapy in that when life is difficult, the power and pleasure of the work itself can carry a client through the pain and provide a feeling of control over the emotional chaos elsewhere. One client, who had been working consistently on his poetry, found it impossible to work after his wife left. The breakdown of the marriage, combined with his inability to work, left him despondent. His therapist said, "You used to sound so excited when you talked about your poems. Do you think there is a connection between the loss of your wife and the loss of your ability to work? Maybe you could try to recapture the excitement you used to have in your work by writing about what you are feeling now. Your marriage isn't the only meaningful thing in your life." This suggestion enabled the client to work on his poems with greater involvement than ever before. The work helped sustain him through the period of emotional distress and gave him a productive way to cope with his loss and pain.

Sometimes artists are afraid not only that therapy will cause the loss of their creativity but also that it will move them toward a conventional mode of life: They will be made to "adjust" to fit society's expectations. But it's a mistake to polarize the possibilities—either total Bohemian unconventionality or crass, unproductive nine-to-five tedium—there is a middle position. As most art is not self-supporting, many artists must hold conventional jobs and are expected to observe conventional hours. At the same time, the work artists really care about is done out of love rather than the expectation of financial remuneration. So the artist must expect at times to feel out of step with the rest of society and must expect to be forced to make compromises between art and survival.

Artists seeking therapy should understand at the start that not all therapists will be sympathetic to their needs. Some may urge them to adopt a conventional way of life. They should question prospective therapists about these attitudes. On the other hand, a therapist's conventional view may have value in encouraging an artist to be appropriately realistic, helping an artist to discover whether he/she is a struggling artist whose talent and effort will eventually bring success or one whose lack of success indicates lack of ability and who should find another line of work. The therapist should be understanding of and sympathetic to the special needs and constraints of the artistic life but at the same time should be able to see when dreams of success have a basis in fact, and when not.

Beginning and established artists have different problems in therapy as well as outside it. (Let us define an **established artist** as someone whose work has been given professional and public validation, *e.g.*, publication in a book or journal with some circulation, a group or one-person show, a public performance.) Established artists are concerned about being unable to repeat their initial success. Many worry that their friends like them only because of their acclaim, not for their own sake, and will vanish if they cease to be successful. They may also worry about the reception of their work in particular negative reviews, and their pain at such reviews may make it difficult for them to work again, fearing their repetition. But established artists will most likely not have the uncertainties over their identity that bring beginning artists to therapy.

An established and successful artist may face the problem of the therapist's envy or excessive gratification at having a famous client. It is often hard to be sure that this is happening. Some signs are: the therapist's tendency to be discouraging about the client's successes, or not being genuinely happy about them; the suggestion by the therapist that it is good therapy that is responsible for the success; the therapist's attempting to create more contact outside the office; and the client's persistent feeling that the therapy is too easy—hard problems are not being examined. These issues should be discussed with the therapist. (Bringing up difficult issues will be discussed in Chapter 5.)

Beginning artists have not yet experienced the community's acceptance of their creative efforts. They want to be artists but don't know whether they have the talent to succeed. Often they fall prey to the pervasive myths about artists' lives: Real artists know they are gifted from the start; real artists think about nothing but creating; real artists remember all their dreams and utilize them in their work; real artists are swept away by inspiration; creativity comes easily to them; real artists must live, and must prefer to live, unconventional and chaotic lives, must experience everything there is to experience, however destructive. A beginning artist whose life does not exemplify these myths may feel confused and hopeless. A good therapist will help make it clear what is myth about the artist's special life, and what is reality.

DEPENDENT PEOPLE

Children and adolescents, who normally enter therapy at the direction of others on whom they are financially dependent and who will be paying for the therapy, present special problems for everyone involved—the parents, the therapist, and the child. (We will be using the term **adolescent** to cover young adults, from roughly ages thirteen to twenty-five, who are still financially dependent on their parents.)

When people pay for something, they often feel entitled to use what they have purchased as they see fit. This may be true with most purchases (and is true when clients pay for their own therapy), but not when client and purchaser are different people. The client is always the person a trustworthy therapist is working for.

For people old enough to make their own decisions on a rational basis (adolescents and adults), the decision whether to enter therapy, which therapist to see, what to work on, and when to terminate, should be left up to them. For children, though, these decisions become the parents' responsibility. Accordingly, for this group, our remarks above on the relationship among client, therapist, and purchaser must be modified. Most often, the decision that a child should be in therapy is made by parents on the basis of their perception of the child's behavior. Either it is disturbing to them (failure in school, bed-wetting), dangerous to society in general (aggressiveness, setting fires), or painful to the child and likely to interfere with the child's successful progress toward maturity (shyness, eating problems, phobias). Before deciding to seek therapy for a child, parents should determine whether their reasons are valid. A valid reason is that the child is clearly unhappy and is not doing well. A less valid reason is that a child is not making *you* happy or living up to *your* expectations. How can you tell which accurately describes the situation? If you can answer "yes" to the following questions, your child is probably basically healthy and therapy is unnecessary—in other words, the problem is yours.

1. Does your child have friends?
2. Does your child usually sleep at night without disturbing dreams?
3. Is your child making satisfactory progress in school?
4. Is your child physically healthy most of the time?
5. Is your child free of debilitating irrational fears?
6. Is your child assertive but not aggressive?
7. Is your child appropriately independent of you?

The symptoms that bring parents to consider therapy generally arise in children as attempts to cope with frightening or disturbing events or continuing difficult situations in their lives. Because so much of children's lives revolves around their families, symptoms are generally indications of difficulties with parents, siblings, or others in the home. This is one reason that the decision to put a child in therapy is so complex and painful for parents: If the child's problems arise from the family milieu, parents feel—rightly or not—that they are responsible, that they have done something wrong, and that the child will tell this and other family secrets to the therapist, who will therefore see (and make the child see) the parents as bad, unloving people. Conscientious parents must overcome these fears, as a child's health and happiness are at stake.

It is helpful to realize that a parent's "responsibility" for a child's distress may be of either of two types. The first involves a disaster that has descended on the family not through anyone's fault: the death of a parent through accident or illness; a parent's loss of a job; the child's own serious illness; and, often, the parents' divorce. If parents can see clearly that they are not to *blame* for what happened, the decision to mitigate the child's suffering through therapy becomes much easier.

On the other hand, there are family problems to which

adults have contributed by deliberate actions that should have been avoided. Examples are: a parent's sexual overtures to a child of any age; the parents' physical or psychological abusiveness to the child or each other; the parents' making impossible demands on the child; a parent's engaging openly in extramarital affairs; severe rivalry between the child and a sibling favored by the parents. If parents recognize situations like these as the causes of the child's distress and symptomatic behavior, their guilt may make it very hard for them to decide to entrust these secrets to an outsider— even a therapist. They should also see that their own burden of guilt and shame for causing their child's distress can only be lightened (and *will* be lightened) by their own ability to take steps toward the child's relief—specifically, to run the risks of having their child see a therapist. Sometimes the symptoms are less the result of the child's bad experience itself than of the child's feeling a need to protect the family's terrible "secret." Therapy, allowing the child to reveal the secret with the certainty that no one but the therapist will find it out, is an important step in helping a child feel less painfully isolated.

How can parents who have decided that their child could profit from therapy find the right therapist? Besides the general recommendations in Chapter 3, there are a few additional considerations. Even more so than for an adult, a child's therapist should appear in an interview as a warm and caring person who can easily establish a rapport with both you and your child without being emotionally effusive or talking down to the child. If after the first interview you feel anger or mistrust toward the therapist, you should look for someone else.

Once a child starts therapy, it may take a while (but no more than three months) for him/her to feel comfortable. The child who wants to terminate therapy earlier should be dissuaded if possible. Children may be uncomfortable in therapy, especially initially, for various reasons. The parents should try to find out what is bothering the child and decide whether to terminate or continue on that basis. If the child seriously mistrusts the therapist, it is probably best to find another therapist. But a child who is uncomfortable about being in therapy itself should be helped to understand that the distress is only temporary and that it is possible and important to overcome it. (If therapy is going well, these feelings will disappear after the initial period.) The child might, for instance, feel that as the only one seeing a therapist, he/she is set apart from the rest of the world. Or the child may be afraid of the memories and emotions that therapy is bringing to the surface, perhaps afraid they make him/her a bad person or afraid that once they are openly acknowledged they will be uncontrollable; or afraid that revealing secrets to an outsider will destroy the family. The child will seldom openly and unambiguously acknowledge any of these fears. But if parents suspect that these concerns are interfering with therapy, they should try to provide reassurance.

After your child has been in therapy for some time, you may expect to see signs of improvement. So you may be disconcerted if, as is frequently the case, the child at first seems to be getting worse: The symptoms are becoming more severe or the child is becoming argumentative or hostile toward you. The therapeutic process itself may create new and deep anxieties to which the worsening behavior is a response. The emotions released in therapy are often brought into extra-therapeutic life—a necessary step in their resolution but hard for everyone involved to live with.

You will want to keep in touch with your child's therapist to see how the therapy is progressing and to discuss problems you are having at home. The therapist may suggest ways to help the therapeutic process. Often these consultations, in person or on the phone, will be quite lengthy, and you should expect to pay for them at the therapist's hourly rate. You may be tempted to try to elicit the child's confidences from the therapist or to justify yourself in the therapist's eyes. You should not be distressed, but rather encouraged, if the therapist avoids being drawn into such discussions. Whether you should expect the therapist to initiate contacts with you depends on the age of your child. It is reasonable for the parents of a younger child to keep in fairly close touch with the therapist about the progress of the therapy, and perhaps at times to explain events in the child's life that are not clear to the therapist. The therapist may also make suggestions to the parents about how to behave with the child.

The parents of an adolescent should expect a more distant relationship with the therapist. Even though they are paying the bills, they should not try to maintain any control over the therapy. They should not interfere with the relationship between client and therapist. They should not question either the child or the therapist about what is happening in therapy. Additionally, they should not volunteer any information about the child or the family: Adolescents can speak for themselves.

The younger child's parents decide whether the child should be in therapy and which therapist to see, but with an adolescent, the problem is more complicated. The adolescent, unlike the child, may have the judgment and maturity to know that help is needed, but the parents must collaborate in the decision with emotional and financial support. Problems can arise if the parents see the adolescent's behavior as a sign of trouble but the adolescent does not: for instance, heavy drug use, frequent truancy, or irresponsible sexual activity. To the parent, these are signs that the adolescent is in trouble and needs help. The latter, though, doesn't necessarily see things this way: Everyone else is doing it, it's fun, and he/she feels no need to talk about it with anyone. If the parent and adolescent have a basically good and open relationship, the parent may be able to persuade the adolescent to see a therapist, and there is a chance therapy will work. But the odds are not very good for real improvement unless the adolescent can be persuaded that the behavior is not as healthy as it seems. (In general, therapy will be unsuccessful unless the client really wants it and feels a need for it.) If an adolescent agrees to see a therapist only in order to please a parent, or to stop the parent from nagging, the prognosis is not good.

To the Adolescent

If you are reading this book, you are probably feeling some distress at home. You may be puzzled by this: Your relationship with your parents has been good until recently. Now it seems as if everything you find enjoyable is objectionable to your parents, and the kind of person they want you to be is nothing like the person you are or would want to be. You would like to please them, but you feel you would have to give up everything that matters to you. Some of this dissatisfaction is typical of adolescence and will go away by itself in time. But sometimes, too, the problems that arise, if they are not dealt with adequately, can cause a great deal of anguish and frequently leave permanent scars and difficulties in later life. Often, the most serious problems cluster around issues of autonomy and identity: The adolescent has to become independent even though this puts him/her in direct and frightening conflict with others in the family. Many of the continuing fights adolescents and their families are involved in—seemingly about, for instance, sex, drugs, success in school or job, choice of friends, sexual preference—are really over autonomy. The conflict arises as much because the parents understand these issues as the adolescent's declaration of independence as because the behavior itself is unacceptable to them.

Therapy can help you with these conflicts in several ways. Your therapist can support your attempts to separate from your parents. Therapy can also help you examine your values and see how well you are working toward achieving them. Below are some questions you can ask yourself to see if therapy would be helpful.

1. Do you sometimes think seriously about suicide?
2. Are you unable to do your work in school?
3. Do you need to take drugs and/or use alcohol?
4. If you are sexually active, is the activity frequently, or usually, without pleasure?
5. If you are sexually active, do you at least sometimes fail to use birth control?
6. Do you hate to be around your house?
7. Do you feel that no one likes you?
8. Do you feel you are worthless?
9. Do you have problems with eating (binges, inability to eat)?
10. Do you have serious problems with sleeping (nightmares, frequent insomnia)?
11. Are you worried or confused about your sexual identity?

If you have answered even one of these questions positively, therapy would be a good idea. As people emotionally and financially dependent on others, adolescents who contemplate therapy face several special problems. If your parents are paying for the therapy (as they probably are), you may be unsure what to expect of the therapist: Can you trust him/her with your confidences? Can you count on him/her to see your side sympathetically when it differs from that of your parents? A competent therapist will see the client as the person he/she is working for regardless of who pays the bills. If the therapist doesn't act that way, you should discuss it, and if things don't get better, find another.

If your parents are reluctant to let you enter therapy, showing them the list above and talking about your answers to it may make your need clearer to them. If you feel certain that you *cannot* reveal your problems to your parents, you should try to find a sympathetic adult who can help financially, emotionally, or both in your search for a therapist: a relative, a teacher or guidance counselor at school, or a friend's parent. Be sure that they will keep your disclosures confidential. If you do not know any sympathetic, knowledgeable, and trustworthy adults, there are publicly funded agencies in most communities (*e.g.*, Planned Parenthood or community mental health centers) that can be of help. You can find them and other sources as well in the Yellow Pages under Social Service Agencies. Once you have made an appointment with a therapist, you may want to bring your list to the initial visit to help clarify what you want to work on.

In the course of your therapy, occasions may arise for consultation between your parents and your therapist. The contact may be initiated by your parents, the therapist, or you. If your parents contact the therapist, he/she should inform you of the content of the discussion as soon as possible. In general, a therapist should permit such consultation only very rarely, in extraordinary situations. A therapist who plans to consult a client's parents should secure the client's permission in advance, after explaining the reasons for the consultation and the topics to be brought up. If you want your therapist to talk to your parents, you should ask yourself why. There are good reasons, and also bad ones. You should not expect your therapist to make your parents into different people. A therapist can change your life only by helping you to change.

MINORITIES

Therapists, like other professionals, have tended to be drawn from those groups in the population who have achieved sociopolitical power. These dominant groups often assume that their ways of behaving, aspirations, and values are the only correct and intelligent ones. Even members of the dominant group who are less ethnocentric are apt to find it difficult to understand someone whose ways of communicating, thinking, and living differ radically from their own. With the best will in the world, such a therapeutic situation is full of dangers and is apt to be more frustrating than helpful.

What sorts of groups are we discussing? The most obvious are those whose native language is not English, so that there may be difficulties even at the level of overt communication. Then there are speakers of English whose socioeconomic background is not middle-class or higher and/or who have less than a college education. Also included are racial minorities, whose experiences with prejudice, as well as whose cultural styles, separate them from the dominant group, whose liberal members may sympathize with stories of discrimination but have never experienced it themselves.

The simplest solution for a member of one of these groups would be to seek out a therapist with a similar background. Unfortunately, because non-dominant groups are severely underrepresented in the profession, such a person may not be available. (Shared ethnic membership, incidentally, is no guarantee of empathetic understanding.) If it is necessary to see a therapist of a different ethnic group from your own, special vigilance is in order, both in the selection of the therapist and in communication in sessions thereafter.

It goes without saying that a therapist should not exhibit any sort of ethnic prejudice—obviously not in the form of explicit slurs but equally not through stereotypical assumptions, positive or negative. The client should not have the feeling that the therapist is perceiving him/her as "one of them," prejudging his/her beliefs, experiences, or problems. Even if it's flattering, the client should not be influenced by a therapist's obvious delight in having a chance to work with someone "exotic." The client, both initially and thereafter, should feel comfortable with the therapist and should feel the therapist can understand reasonably well—and if not, can acknowledge ignorance and ask for explanations. (This is always meritorious in a therapist, but it becomes increasingly crucial the less client and therapist share a common set of assumptions.)

In the course of therapy, the client will have to remain unusually alert for miscommunications, things that are not understood as intended by either party. (Technically, this is the therapist's job, but as catching and interpreting misunderstandings tends to be the business of non-dominant groups, the therapist may not be as perceptive in this area as is desirable.) If therapist and client can remain open-minded and willing to learn about both themselves and each other, the therapeutic experience can be unusually rewarding for both.

GAY PEOPLE

Conflict or confusion about sexual preference often leads people to consider therapy. Younger people especially may be uncertain about their sexual preference and may want a therapist to help resolve it. People may know they are gay and want to change, or know they are gay and be content with that but want help in coming out of the closet and coping with the changes and disruptions that may cause. Finally, being attracted to people of both the same and the opposite sex may create even more severe problems than being unequivocally gay. While some concerns about the choice of therapist are the same for gays and heterosexuals, there also are some special considerations.

If sexual preference is a primary issue, it is of the utmost importance that the therapist not have a bias against gays or see homosexuality as an illness that successful therapy will cure. You should question a prospective therapist about this and be convinced that it is not the therapist's point of view that therapeutic success depends upon your "going straight." Your therapist should be reasonably tolerant of a variety of gay ways of life. An appropriate therapist is one who will help you determine what is right and comfortable for *you*.

You may wonder how important it is whether your therapist is gay. You should remember that you are entering therapy in part to deal with your sexuality but even more to explore all aspects of your thoughts and feelings. So it is most important that the therapist you choose be someone, whether gay or straight, whom you can work with and trust.

PEOPLE OVER FIFTY

People over fifty may feel that as older people, they should be experienced enough not to need guidance and help. They may feel, too, that it's too late for them to change, that their lives have to go on as they always have. They may also worry if their therapist is younger than they are: Can they tell their problems to someone the age of their children? But these assumptions are fallacious. Therapy is equally useful for older and younger people, although their needs and goals may be somewhat different. It's better to change late in life than never.

What can the older person hope to accomplish in therapy? Certain things are inevitable as people get older: diminished physical power, the loss of friends through death, fewer possibilities for fresh starts, one's own illness and eventual death. People over fifty also often have to adjust to new relationships with their children, which alter the old balance of power. This period of life may be a time of reflection upon one's accomplishments and failures, and regret for what might have been.

Therapy can help you discover which changes are inevitable in the aging process and which are limitations that *you* are imposing. These feelings can be dealt with by a competent therapist, who can help you come to terms with them and feel more resolved.

How will you find this competent therapist? In general, the problem is the same as for anyone else, but there are a few special considerations. There is a reasonable likelihood that some of the therapists you interview will be younger than you. This may at first cause you some concern: Can younger people understand the problems their elders have, problems they themselves have never encountered? Will a younger therapist be able to understand and respect the beliefs of an older person? Can an older person comfortably receive help from a younger person? It is not to be expected or desired that even the most competent therapist will be able to ignore differences in age (in either direction); rather, the competent therapist will always be aware of the differences and will be able to put this awareness to use in the therapy. It's easier for a therapist to be encouraging to a younger client, who so clearly has many possibilities still open, but a sensitive therapist is able to see older clients in the same light and communicate that to them. A therapist who has basically positive attitudes toward life can communicate best with any client, but especially with the older client.

Especially for the older client, therapy should never release emotions that are too painful to tolerate. Loss, sorrow, and guilt are especially apt to get out of control for older clients. Competent therapists can allow clients gradually to confront these feelings without forcing them to assimilate them all at once. You should feel that your therapist is in control and allowing you to experience these painful confrontations at a pace you find bearable. The discomfort that is inevitable at times in any good therapy should be balanced by an increasing ability to cope with emotional material. If your therapy does no more than remind you of what you can no longer do, what you did wrong, and what you wish you had accomplished, without the encouragement of hope and achievement, it is not good therapy and you should look for a new therapist.

WOMEN

For the past few decades, the roles and expectations of women have been changing radically. In most ways, this has been advantageous: New possibilities have opened up, and women are now freer to explore and experiment. But with this new array of choices come difficult decisions and new responsibilities, and the new possibilities coexist with old stereotypes. So women often feel a great deal of conflict: What can they do? What should they want to do? Can they manage two very different roles—say, professional woman and mother—successfully? Can they be both lovable and businesslike?

The first responsibility for women now is to make a choice. With the bewildering array of choices and the often unclear reasons for each, it can be helpful for a woman to talk to someone outside her circle of friends and family. A therapist can help a woman find what is appropriate for her. But she should be careful: There are therapists who see their work as reinforcing the current status quo, making their clients "adjust," and suggesting to them that if they do not fit themselves into whatever model the therapist sees as appropriately feminine, they are failures as women and as human beings. To become involved with such a therapist is counterproductive and antitherapeutic. A woman should be very clear that her therapist sees her, first of all, as a human being and *not* as a member of a group who must play a particular, preconceived role (whatever that role may be).

In an initial interview, one woman talked to a prospective therapist about her uncertainties about her career and her lack of self-confidence. The therapist seemed to her warm and intuitive, and she was favorably impressed. But as she was getting up to leave, he said to her, "Of course, the most important thing for you is to have a husband and children." The woman realized that a therapist with these unexamined prejudices could not understand the conflicts she was trying to resolve. And despite his many good qualities, she decided to see someone else.

This woman was fortunate that the therapist's bias was clearly revealed before she could be injured by it. More often, such biases are hidden. Therefore a client should remain alert for subtle cues to the therapist's hidden belief system and unexamined preconceptions.

Most often these preconceptions concern a woman's "normal" role as a mother: Any indication that she is not willing to sacrifice herself and her interests to her children is seen as a symptom that she is not a good woman. If you bring up negative feelings about children—actual or prospective—the therapist shouldn't regularly take the child's side, making you feel guilty. Instead, you should be encouraged to believe that being a person with less than unlimited resources of patience and love is perfectly normal. Also helpful is a therapist who can help you set limits with members of your family, help you discover why you feel you have to be a perfect wife and mother, what you fear if you are not, or what the reward is to be if you succeed. In other words, rather than applauding and supporting every indication of your need to be everything to your family, the therapist should be helping you define your own needs and desires and showing you how to justify and fully accept them.

Nor should the therapist discourage your exploration of your feelings about having children (or, if you have them, the feelings you have toward them). As a woman approaches forty, the question of whether or not to have a child must be resolved. The woman who feels that this is not something she needs or wants to think about is probably avoiding the issue, and a sensitive therapist will help her recognize its importance to her—without, however, pushing her to make the decision in either way.

Very often the surface problems that bring a woman to therapy are related to something more disturbing at a deeper level. Fears of, and anger toward, men; problems with sexuality; and low self-esteem may be based on early forced sexual encounters—more often than had been believed—with older men in their families, or sometimes friends of the family. These experiences, remembered or not, create a wide swath of destruction through many aspects of a woman's life. A therapist who recognizes that such early traumatic relationships are the source of a client's difficulty, and can help the client work through the pain to recapture the early memories and mitigate their destructive power, can provide a great deal of relief and can help the client to live a much more productive life. A therapist who appears skeptical at the outset of a client's reports of such events is a therapist not to trust—and not to see.

We have seen that certain groups have special needs and concerns that make their job in finding and selecting a therapist more difficult. But for all of them, the right therapist will make the experience rewarding. And if they have had to go through unusual trouble in finding the right person to work with, it is very possible that as a result their experience in therapy will be unusually productive.

SUGGESTED READING

Artists

Milner, Marion, *On Not Being Able to Paint*. New York, International Universities Press, 1957.

Rothenberg, Albert, *The Emerging Goddess.* Chicago, University of Chicago Press, 1979.

Children

Heffner, Elaine, *Mothering.* New York, Doubleday, 1980.
Kaplan, Louise J., *Oneness and Separateness.* New York, Simon and Schuster, 1978.

Adolescents

Laing, R. D., and Esterson, A., *Sanity, Madness and the Family.* Baltimore, Pelican Books, 1970.
York, Phyllis, and Wachtel, David, *Toughlove.* New York, Bantam, 1983.

People Over Fifty

Frym, Gloria, *Second Stories: Conversations with Women Whose Artistic Careers Began After 35.* San Francisco, Chronicle Books, 1979.
Yalom, Irvin D., *Existential Psychotherapy.* New York, Basic Books, 1980.

Women

(See entries for Heffner, and Laing and Esterson above.)
Peterson, Nancy L., *Our Lives for Ourselves—Women Who Have Never Married.* New York, Putnam, 1981.
Rapoport, Rhona; Strelitz, Robert N.; and Strelitz, Ziona, *Fathers, Mothers and Society.* New York, Basic Books, 1977.

Part Two

HOW THERAPY WORKS

CHAPTER 5

The Quality of the Relationship

The therapeutic relationship is an intimate one in which both participants have feelings toward each other. The therapist should feel benevolent and caring toward the client—nothing stronger. The therapist should not, for example, respond to a client with anger or desire. On the other hand, the client from time to time may find himself/herself feeling these stronger emotions for the therapist and may be troubled about them—especially the almost inevitable sexual feelings. This anxiety arises out of confusion between what is appropriate in ordinary relationships and in psychotherapy. Ordinarily, when we feel strongly attracted to someone, we act on it: We flirt, we hint, we proposition. But usually we do not discuss the feelings with their object. In therapy, however, you can acknowledge the existence of such feelings without acting on them, and moreover you can use them as a way of examining your sexuality. In therapy, although these feelings are real, they are not taken at face value. If you have brought up these sexual feelings (as you should), your therapist should be able to discuss them and not act on them or make fun of them. If your therapist treats your feelings dispassionately, you may feel hurt and rejected. You are not used to having your most personal disclosures treated this way. But you have to recall that you are in therapy to discover the *origins* of your sexual responses, not to repeat what you have been doing all your life, probably unhappily.

Your feelings for your therapist may become the most intense and important ones in your life. This is normal. You may even worry about how you can ever end this relationship. But when you are ready to end the therapy, you'll be much better able than now to share your feelings with someone other than the therapist. Also, you'll have learned to see your therapist more realistically, and the passion of hero worship will have subsided. You will be left with feelings of friendliness and gratitude, and your therapist, with warm memories and genuine caring.

You may wonder how openness and self-disclosure are possible in therapy, especially if you ordinarily have misgivings about revealing yourself. How can you dare to open yourself up to someone else, especially someone who doesn't reciprocate? How do you know the therapist won't use what you say against you in some way? Won't think you're bizarre—or just ridiculous? It isn't easy, but most people do learn, however slowly, how to be open, through the development of a feeling that has been given the name **basic trust**.

Basic trust is the cornerstone of the therapeutic process. It is the feeling that another person means well toward you and will not do you harm. Therefore you can be fully yourself in that person's presence. Normally people develop this kind of trust in infancy toward their mothers. If this fails to happen, they will suffer in later relationships from unnecessary suspicion and jealousy. People often enter therapy with problems having to do with lack of basic trust, although they may not then be aware that this is the source of their problems. The therapeutic relationship seeks to repair this early injury. Therapy both teaches and depends upon basic trust.

At first you may find it hard to be fully trusting in therapy. Your therapist should be able to discover and comment on any lack of trust, and you should try to trust him/her enough to explore it. In the very process of discussing your lack of trust and seeing that your therapist doesn't reject you because of it, you are building trust. If you feel uncomfortable at any point in these conversations, you should try to discuss the source of your feelings and their seriousness. The natural discomfort that comes from any confrontation and self-disclosure should lessen after a while. Your therapist should not avoid dealing with these feelings by maintaining silence, changing the subject, or telling you not to worry.

Trust must exist on both sides. Your therapist has to believe in your good intentions and consider you a worthwhile person. This doesn't mean approving of everything you do or say. You also should have the feeling that your therapist thinks of you as unique and not as an illustration of some theory or diagnostic category. After a few months in therapy, you should be able to see how much credence your therapist gives to your reports of real-life events. You should be given the benefit of the doubt: Everything you claim to be real should be so treated by the therapist unless and until there are ironclad arguments for treating it as fantasy. There is nothing so demoralizing, so disruptive of trust, as to be disbelieved when telling the truth. People do, of course, sometimes reconstruct events in their past in ways that did not happen. But you cannot trust a therapist who blatantly mistrusts you—even in the name of therapeutic theory. And even when suggesting that your recollection may be a fantasy, a therapist should do so with respect for you and should not give you the feeling of being accused of deceit or irrationality. If you ever sense that your statements are not being treated with respect, you must discuss your feelings with your therapist.

You may wonder how you can accurately discern your therapist's attitude. There are no specific words or actions to watch for: As is the case so often, you must rely on your intuition. When you talk about real-life events, you have to feel that your therapist is with you, believing what you are saying. In general, except where quite disturbed people are concerned, events reported as happening are almost always factually true. It's their interpretation, the motivation behind them, their relation to other events in a client's life, as well as the client's responsibility for causing them, that require an attitude of "benevolent skepticism" on the therapist's part.

While being benevolent, the therapist must remain vigilant for the client's blind spots, as they often provide clues to how he/she sees the world. One client was talking to her therapist about an incident in the supermarket that morning. In response to her question, the checker had snapped impatiently at her. She saw this incident, she said, as evidence that she was invariably mistreated and victimized by everyone in her life. The therapist listened sympathetically: It was clear, she said, that the client had been hurt. But more was needed. "I can see that you're hurt," the therapist said. "But let's set that aside for a moment while we look at some questions. How busy was the checker? Was she talking to someone else at the time? . . ." The therapist was trying to help her client perceive that there were things she hadn't been aware of—characteristic blind spots. By asking questions that forced the client to rethink and re-evaluate events, the therapist was teaching her to understand that some of her difficulties with people arose because she didn't reflect on their needs before confronting them with her needs. Now the client will be able to question herself, when similar incidents arise in the future, and eventually to stop the behavior that brings her trouble. The therapist didn't doubt the client's story but only her perception of the reasons behind the events reported.

If your therapist generally treats your factual reports as fantasy without giving you good reasons for doing so, your therapy is severely endangered. You cannot trust someone who is that suspicious of you, however well-armed the therapist may be with theoretical arguments for the suspicion. If you feel your therapist, in exploring the underlying meanings and causes of events in your life, is using interpretation to attack you and erode your self-confidence (even if the interpretations themselves seem unimpeachable), the therapeutic relationship is similarly in trouble. If you feel anything other than a full member of a partnership based on mutual good will, a partnership whose function is to help you understand your mind and life, you should be very careful about continuing. Should you have doubts, the first step is to raise them explicitly with your therapist. If he/she shows any reluctance to explore these issues, or tells you without adequate reasons that you're "distorting," "resisting," etc., it's time to think about ending the therapy. Beware of the use of jargon like this to embarrass you into obedience. Your self-esteem and sense of personal integrity and reliability are too precious, and perhaps too fragile, to risk.

We have been talking about problems that arise within the therapeutic framework itself: difficulties in actually doing therapy. Problems can also arise if either of the participants steps out of that frame of reference, contaminating the therapeutic relationship. Because this relationship is so special, to treat it, at the participants' convenience, like friendship is to greatly weaken its power to create change. Therefore any attempt, by either participant, to redefine the relationship, tempting as it may sometimes seem, is a serious error.

There is a difference, however, between extra-therapeutic contact initiated by the client and that initiated by the therapist. The client, especially at the beginning when the rules are not yet clear, can be expected to err in this direction and can expect to be dissuaded (gently and kindly) by the therapist if the contact is inappropriate. Examples of acceptable extra-therapeutic contacts are: the client's showing his/her writing to the therapist, or the therapist's attending a client's performance. These have to do with the client's work and need not involve the therapist in the client's daily personal life. On the other hand, the client might invite the therapist to a party, in which case the therapist ought to refuse. Going to a client's party would force the therapist to encounter many of the client's friends and would reveal the nature of his/her relationship with the client. Likewise the client would be forced to encounter the therapist in a new framework, perhaps behaving in unexpected ways that might be disturbing.

For the therapist to initiate changes in the relationship is an even more serious violation. The therapist then is using the client for his/her personal gratification or self-aggrandizement. Flattering as it may be to you if the therapist treats you in this way, you have to recognize and resist his/her behavior as counter-therapeutic. If the therapist persists, consider ending the therapy.

Additionally, you should beware if your therapist seeks to initiate contact of any kind with you outside the therapeutic setting, from inviting you to lunch to talking to you at length at a party. More serious is an attempt to initiate a sexual relationship: a kiss, a hug, or anything more. Other signs of exploitation include a therapist's changing the rules unilaterally without negotiation. Or the therapist might start talking to you about his/her own problems when they have no reference to your needs.

After some time in therapy, one client noticed that her therapist was gradually spending more and more of the therapeutic hour talking about his own life and problems in ways she could not connect with her own concerns. Then one day as she entered his office he said to her, "Let's switch roles today. There are some things I want to talk to you about." For the next fifty minutes he proceeded to tell her the details of his childhood, interspersed with tears. The client was flattered that he would consider her worthy of his confidence but at the same time terribly confused. Who was the therapist here? How could she be open and direct with him after this, when anything she said might cause him distress? Now she felt she had to take care of him—and still pay him his regular fee. Although the client stayed in therapy with this man, she found it impossible to make progress.

Should you find yourself in such a position, the solution is obvious. You should terminate your therapy immediately. But these kinds of dramatic situations are usually preceded by indications that the therapist is losing control. Whenever you sense that the therapist's contributions don't relate to what you have been discussing, ask, "What does this have to do with me?" The therapist might have had a perfectly good reason for the apparent irrelevancy, in which case the explanation will help you to understand the process better.

A therapist who cancels appointments frequently, or displays inappropriate emotions (such as anger) toward you, is also exploiting you by using your therapeutic hour to provide for his/her personal needs. We aren't saying that the therapist should suppress all emotion—for instance, it is appropriate for the therapist to cry when particularly moved by something you have said. This is not a sign of lack of control or professionalism on the therapist's part but an expression of humanness and caring. But the therapist's emotions should not discourage, or take precedence over, your own expressions of feeling. They should work toward helping you understand yourself. It's your hour, not the therapist's.

If you are concerned that any of these forms of exploitation is occurring, but you are not sure, one way to clarify things is to get a second opinion. Make an appointment with another therapist, explaining when you call that you want a consultation to discuss problems you are encountering with your therapist. You should be prepared to give a short history of the therapeutic relationship, describing succinctly what is happening that is causing you distress. It should take no more than one session to get an opinion. Don't worry about being disloyal to the therapist: Your psychological health is at stake.

Because the therapeutic process is new to you, and the therapist is a figure of special authority and mystery, it will probably be hard for you to figure out, at the beginning, whether your relationship with the therapist is a good one. But part of what you learn in therapy is how to accurately recognize your feelings toward others and those of others toward you, as well as how to discuss them and get conflicts resolved. Moreover, your therapeutic experience cannot be satisfactory if you suppress confusion, anger, or resentment.

Therefore you should use the following checklists as guides to help you formulate and evaluate your responses to the therapeutic relationship, in order to determine whether it is meeting your needs. In therapy that is expected to last a year or more, you should use these checklists fairly early—between the third and sixth months—and from time to time thereafter, whenever you feel any uncertainty.

Checklist 5A

YOUR THERAPIST'S FEELINGS TOWARD YOU

1. Do you feel your therapist likes you? (2)
2. Does your therapist treat you like a unique individual rather than a representative of a psychological "category"? (1)
3. Does your therapist usually seem interested in you and what you say? (1)
4. Can you generally count on your therapist to keep appointments? (2)
5. Does your therapist restrict his/her expression of emotions to what is relevant and helpful to you? (1)

SCORING: Score each question according to the number in parentheses. If you've answered "no" to questions rated 1, raise these issues with the therapist. If he/she seems open and able to change, give him/her another chance. If you have answered "no" to either question rated 2, you should ask yourself whether to continue therapy with this person. If you have answered both 2-rated questions "no," leave. If your therapist will not discuss any of the issues raised in this checklist, you should also consider ending the therapy.

Checklist 5B

YOUR ROLE IN THE PROCESS

1. When the therapist talks about himself/herself, is it generally relevant to you? (1)
2. If the therapist changes any of the rules you agreed upon, do you have a chance to discuss it? (2)
3. If you disagree with the therapist about an interpretation, does the therapist listen to you respectfully? (2)
4. If you criticize something he/she says, does the therapist treat criticism as part of the process rather than as unreasonable behavior or irrationality? (2)
5. Can you tell the therapist when you think he/she is judging you unfairly? (2)
6. Can you tell the therapist you are afraid to raise certain issues? (1)
7. Do you feel the therapist can discuss all aspects of the therapeutic relationship with you, without anxiety or hostility? (2)
8. Does your therapist refrain from initiating contact with you outside the hour? (2)
9. Does your therapist show appropriately warm and caring responses to you? (1)

SCORING: You should be able to answer "yes" to all questions. For those rated 1, the therapy may be able to survive with only one or two "no" answers. If, however, you have answered "no" to more than two 1-rated questions or to *any* 2-rated questions, you should ask yourself whether this relationship is really therapeutic for you.

If you have any "no's" on either checklist, it is your responsibility to discuss them with your therapist. This is difficult: You may not be sure that your perceptions are accurate, and even if you are, you don't want to bring up issues that may impair an important relationship that already is troubled. But if you don't discuss these problems as soon as you are aware of them, they will only get worse over time. Letting bad communication continue reinforces it, making it impossible to change, and keeps the therapy from working as well as it should. There is no way you can confront your therapist without anxiety, but you will feel better if you realize that you're doing what is appropriate.

Despite your resolution to discuss problems in the relationship with your therapist, you may feel uncertain how to go about it. Even with friends we tend to avoid confrontation, so we don't know how to do it in a non-threatening, non-apologetic way. You wonder whether you should be direct or not, and how you should approach each point.

But these are mere technical details. Far outweighing them is the fear of confronting the therapist—the sort of fear that makes usually articulate people forget all the words they know or decide that the problem isn't really worth the trouble (knowing perfectly well that it is). One way to make the confrontation easier is to imagine it in advance, perhaps as a sort of scenario. The real scene, of course, won't work exactly like your fantasy, but the feeling you'll get from rehearsal—that you *do* have something important to say and *do* know the right words to say it with—will sustain you through the reality.

First, imagine a fairly easy situation, say, question 2 on Checklist 5B (If the therapist changes any of the rules you agreed upon, do you have a chance to discuss it?).

You: There is something I have been unclear about, and I wanted to bring it up with you so that we'd know where we both stand.

THERAPIST: Hmm . . .

YOU: At our first session, when we discussed the rules, you said that if I canceled a session at least twenty-four hours in advance, I wouldn't have to pay for it. But I got my first bill from you the other day, and I saw that I was being charged for a session I had canceled. See, here, September 28? And I'm sure I told you about it at my last session before that. Did I misunderstand you, or is there an error on the bill?

THERAPIST: Hmm . . . yes . . . I *do* remember our discussing cancellations, and I agree that I told you about the twenty-four-hour policy. But I don't recall your telling me about the cancellation, and I kept that hour open, so I have to charge you for it.

YOU: I *know* I told you. Perhaps it was your mistake.

THERAPIST: I really don't remember, but I'll tell you what I'll do. I'll split the charge for that hour with you. In the future I would appreciate your making sure that I give you some verbal acknowledgment that I've heard you.

A more difficult situation would arise in response to a "no" on question 4, Checklist 5B (If you criticize something he/she says, does the therapist treat criticism as part of the process rather than as unreasonable behavior or irrationality?), where emotions rather than finances are involved. This will be harder for both of you, but there are ways to get through it gracefully.

YOU: Last week, when I told you the dream about my mother and the anaconda, I was disturbed at your interpretation. You said you were the mother and I was the anaconda, and I wanted to eat you up. I said that didn't seem right to me, that you're always turning my associations into a desire to possess you sexually. You said it wasn't the client's job to make interpretations. Of course, I realize I am here to learn from you, but one thing I know I need to learn is to recognize my real feelings. I feel I was making a valid point, and you brushed it aside. I was hurt and disappointed.

THERAPIST: But I really see your associations that way.

YOU: What if I see them in another way? If your interpretations don't work for me? Can we look at the dream again, to see if there is an interpretation that feels right for both of us? I don't want to accept interpretations that don't seem right to me.

In both scenarios:

1. You state what happened as you remember it, refreshing the therapist's mind and making sure you are in agreement about what happened.
2. You state clearly and succinctly the reason that you are upset.
3. You give the therapist some kind of "out," a way to yield to your view of things without a total loss of face. Begin your question with "Maybe I didn't understand," or "We may have been unclear about . . ."
4. You remain calm and objective.

We have spent so much time talking about things that can go wrong in therapy that by now you may be anxious and despondent. You may even be wondering whether the benefits of therapy are worth the risks. But remember that we have concentrated hcrc on some of the worst possibilities so that if they happen, you won't feel isolated and alone but will have the tools to deal with them. If you have chosen a good therapist, the most serious problems won't arise, and the lesser ones can be negotiated. If you have made a bad choice, you'll have discovered it and gotten out early enough to avoid damage. But don't expect all these calamities to occur.

Certainly the positive aspects of a good therapeutic relationship outweigh the risks. In such a relationship you'll find acceptance, warmth, and sharing—and the exciting feeling of being part of a team working together to learn something important. The feeling that you and your therapist are truly engaged in collaboration can itself enrich your life and help you make the changes you want to make.

CHAPTER 6

Power: The Crux of the Therapeutic Relationship

O ne of the most important things to learn in therapy is how to use power in productive ways. How easy it is for a client to learn this depends in part on the therapist's feeling about power. But in order to understand the function of power in therapy, we have to ask what power is and how it is used and abused in the real world. In therapy, clients have to learn how to be powerful: how to identify their power and use it appropriately, for themselves and others. To consider power so important will be shocking to many readers, who have learned to despise people who are obsessed with power, or "power-hungry." But this reaction is based on a definition of power very different from the one we are developing here.

People enter therapy feeling helpless and therefore assuming that in order to get what they need from others, they must resort to manipulation or coercion, because they don't have the right or the strength to make direct and explicit statements. Sometimes they are so afraid of refusal or rejection that they will not even risk asking but will nonetheless be disappointed if others don't magically guess their wishes and fulfill them. Sometimes these illegitimate strategies get people what they want; more often, not. But even when they are ostensibly successful, they are dangerous in the long run. The users of illegitimate means feel false to themselves and degraded; the people against whom they are directed feel used and are apt to be hostile to the users in the future. To use indirect or coercive tactics is to establish adversarial relationships that are bound to explode or fall apart.

Power of some sort is central to all relationships. But because people are accustomed to thinking of power as either manipulation or coercion, and because people have an image of themselves and their society as egalitarian, discussion of power makes them uncomfortable: They try to pretend that it is not an issue.

In fact, contemporary American society treats power as a taboo topic, in a manner in many ways reminiscent of the Victorian attitude toward sexuality. The Victorians had sex—otherwise we would not be here. But they could not openly acknowledge that they had sexual needs and that their relationships were motivated to some degree by these needs. The hypocrisy necessitated by this attitude led people to keep secrets from themselves as well as everyone else, and these secrets led to the symptoms that brought people into psychoanalysis. By encouraging his patients to be honest with themselves and undo the taboo, Freud relieved many of their symptoms. It was not so much the revelation of sexuality itself that cured but the process of saying what had previously been unsayable and realizing that one was not a terrible person for being able to say such things about oneself. It was a sense, too, that one was not alone in possessing these desires; they were shared by everyone else. What everybody knew was going on could now be openly acknowledged.

Today we have much the same feeling about power. Just as *sex* was a dirty word to the Victorians, so *power* is to us. We all know that power is instrumental in our relationships and that we need to feel powerful in our lives, but we can't say so: We have to think of ourselves as people who are only interested in equality and friendliness. Anything that contradicts this image we do not acknowledge or talk about. Therefore, just as the Victorians developed symptoms to express indirectly the sexuality that couldn't be expressed openly, we have developed symptoms as ways of dealing with the need for power that we cannot honestly acknowledge. So while we seldom see the hysteria and obsessional neurosis that Freud encountered, we are hardly free of psychological distress.

Of course, we are not in exactly the same position the Victorians were in before Freud. Freud taught people to be alert to the possibility of ulterior motives and hidden reasons for actions and beliefs. He taught people how to engage in therapy, how to work on their minds, and he offered the possibility of change through insight. But the methods he devised were most useful for a society such as his and for a clientele whose reasons for entering therapy sprang largely from sexual repression. In Victorian Europe, power imbalances, unlike sexual urges, were taken for granted and openly acknowledged. Hence traditional psychoanalysis, in which the analyst had power over his patient and made explicit use of it, worked well in that culture and did not cause distress or exacerbate symptoms. But today, utilizing the same techniques does not work as well. Anyone with a modicum

of psychological health will rebel at being perceived as inferior in every way to the therapist; further, this assumption
will interfere with the development of autonomy.

Society as a whole has, of course, changed greatly since
the turn of the century. Because Freud brought to light new
areas of the human psyche, we are much freer than our
forebears. We are accustomed to talking about many of our
needs and fears—sexual and otherwise. Topics once strictly
forbidden in polite society are the common coin of the cock-
tail party now. Only someone who has spent the last eighty
years in a cave doesn't know that every boy wants to sleep
with his mother. So the shock value of sexual enlighten-
ment, which itself was responsible for a good part of therapeutic efficacy, is much reduced for us. Unfortunately,
many conventional therapists have not fully achieved this
new understanding and speak to their clients of sexual matters as if these were still the shocking revelations that make
therapy effective. The result is to diminish the therapists'
credibility, not to mention the effectiveness of the therapy.

What is new and shocking today is the revelation that
the desire for power underlies many of our social interactions. Therefore it is the power dynamic of the therapeutic
situation that is the basis for change, because it mirrors the
most crucial problems in the outside world. But this fact
necessitates not only a new look at the content of the psychotherapeutic session but also a reinterpretation of the
relationship between the participants: Power becomes the
dominant issue, whether this is openly acknowledged or not.
The difference is that if it is openly acknowledged, it is a positive force for change; left a dirty secret, it poisons the therapeutic relationship and keeps the client stuck in the unproductive old patterns.

There are at least two reasons that people are afraid of
acknowledging their potential for being powerful. First, this

society prefers to think of itself, inaccurately, as egalitarian; to think of anyone (including oneself) as "powerful" suggests that that person is capable of, and perhaps desirous of, upsetting that appearance of equality. Second, to be powerful is to take full responsibility for one's thoughts, words, needs, and actions. The person who has brought events about takes the credit if they work out well, the blame if they go badly. A person with healthy self-esteem will feel that there is a reasonable chance things will go well and will gladly take the responsibility, with the expectation of getting credit for a good outcome afterward. But for people whose self-esteem is more fragile, the possibility of disaster always looms large, and taking responsibility necessarily suggests taking the blame later. (Our language reinforces this equation between accountability and blame: We use *responsible* to mean both "accountable" and "blameworthy." *He is responsible for that* can mean either, "He is the one who did that," or, "He is to blame for that.") If people can manipulate events, they can later claim they weren't really responsible and so are blameless. Therefore people must feel good about themselves before they can feel truly powerful and must *feel* powerful before they can *be* powerful.

Power has been variously defined, either as the ability to make people do what they wouldn't otherwise do or as the ability to get things done. Neither of these definitions covers the way we want to use the word. The first suggests coercion, a use of power that is rightly condemned; the second, accomplishing *things:* We are more interested in working toward feeling stronger in relationships with *people* (although competence in work is a part of what we are talking about). From this perspective, we can define **power** as *taking responsibility for what you say, what you do, and what you think*. When you are willing and able to do this, you can be clear and direct in what you tell people: You can be informative about yourself and your needs, allowing people to know you. To do this, you have to believe that people will want to know the "real" you and they will then want to try what you suggest. Failure to believe in yourself encourages, and in fact necessitates, manipulative behavior.

To be truly powerful, you must be direct. You start by saying what you want and whether you are willing to compromise. You must believe that you're entitled to what you are asking for. Whether a statement is appropriately powerful or not depends not so much on the actual *form* of your statement but on the *feelings* and *intentions* that underlie it. An utterance, in other words, may be ambiguous, but the speaker's intention may be clarified by tone of voice or facial expression. A statement is coercive if the speaker's object was to get his/her own way or to show who's boss.

To avoid some of the bad connotations of "power," let's call this way of feeling and acting **autonomy.** From the description, autonomy may sound to you like an easy and risk-free way to behave. But it is not without its hazards. Refusing to go along with other people's wishes sometimes alienates them. But those relationships that are based on autonomy are the most rewarding.

People resort to **manipulation** because they see themselves, realistically or not, as weak. There is always an implicit threat behind manipulative behavior. But it is implicit: The manipulator doesn't take responsibility for deliberately carrying it out. Manipulation may be done through verbal hints or non-verbally, *e.g.*, by crying, getting sick, or withdrawing from the interaction.

Coercion, the most obvious of illegitimate power tactics, is only successful when there is a real discrepancy in power between the individuals: parent and child, student and teacher, or sometimes, husband and wife. Someone who has total economic control over another person can use it coercively, as can someone (like a parent) who has great emotional control. Threatening to withdraw from someone what that person needs in order to survive (physically or emotionally) is not unlike holding a gun to someone's head.

Someone who is capable of coercion may appear strong, even worthy of being emulated. But there is a paradox to coercion: The coercer is, at heart, afraid and therefore weak. The coercer really doesn't feel entitled or legitimate, does not anticipate getting his/her way. Coercion comes from a fear of being wrong—the very antithesis of self-esteem—and its continued use is corrosive to self-confidence. Once coercion enters a relationship, it must be continued and escalated, if only to (falsely) persuade the coercer of his/her power. Hence the coercer *and* the coerced are bound inextricably to this form of relationship. Both are imprisoned, and both learn to hate and resent themselves and each other.

In other words, both manipulation and coercion depend in their different ways on getting other people to make one (temporarily) feel strong. True autonomy comes from within. The first two attempt to use external evidence of worth to shore up tenuous self-esteem; the last uses real internal strength to persuade others to a course of action that is beneficial for everyone.

Consider how the following imaginary situation would be handled through each of these strategies: A woman has just learned that her husband is having an affair. In a *manipulative* strategy, after the woman finds out, she phones her best friend and tells her about her husband's infidelity, and says that she intends to swallow a bottle of sleeping pills. She does so and leaves her husband a note telling him she's killing herself over his affair. Meanwhile, the friend calls an ambulance, and the wife is brought to the hospital, where her stomach is pumped. Her husband gets home and finds the suicide note and a message from the friend that his wife is in the emergency room. He rushes there, overcome with guilt, finds his wife recovering, and pledges to end the affair. The wife has gotten what she wanted—but at a high cost and only for a while. The real difficulty in the marriage has not been dealt with effectively, and this technique won't work again. Worse, the woman has gained her purpose through a show of weakness. She got what she wanted because she was "sick," "crazy," "out of control." In the future, no one will take her seriously—not even she herself.

In a *coercive* strategy, the woman finds a way to threaten real harm to her husband. She knows he's been cheating on his income taxes. She tells him that if the affair continues, she will report him anonymously to the IRS. He knows that if she carries out her threat (and he believes she will), he will probably go to prison, and his livelihood will be destroyed. So he ends the affair, but the marriage is in even more jeopardy, and he has learned only to be more careful in his future indiscretions and less open with his wife. The only means she'll have to get him to do anything in the future are similarly coercive—he will never do anything out of love.

To act *autonomously* in this situation, the woman has to make a decision about her marriage: either that it is basically sound and worth working on to preserve, or that it is dead and therefore should be ended. If she makes the former choice, she has to know that she is staying in the marriage out of love and commitment, not out of fear that she could not survive without a man. Next she must confront her husband directly, making reference to both of their needs and feelings—not playing on his or her vulnerabilities. She must be willing to risk the pain and hurt that could come of exposing her feelings to someone who has already hurt her. She says to him: "I know you are having an affair.

It is hurting me a lot, because I believe in monogamy in marriage. I can only stay with you if you end the affair and don't have others. I love you very much, but these are the only terms that are acceptable to me. Are you willing to accept them?" She must be clear and direct about her needs and her limits. This makes her more vulnerable if her husband wants to misuse her confidence. But at the same time it gives her strength: She knows what she wants and who she is, and she has made her feelings clear to him. The direct confrontation also gives her an opportunity to see what kind of person her husband is—if he ends the affair, she can be sure he is doing it out of love and commitment to the marriage, not out of fear or guilt. He is able to take responsibility for his behavior, because she did so. In the future neither one can say, "You made me do it, so I didn't mean it." They both have made a free choice to preserve the marriage.

There is a sharp distinction between autonomy and (something often confused with it) **control.** Control is the aim of manipulation and coercion—it is non-autonomous, because it focuses on keeping *someone else* under control. This saps the controller's energy and fills him/her with fear: What if the other person escapes control—what will be left in the relationship?

We are using *control* to mean what is often meant by *power:* the restriction of other people's options. People frequently don't realize that by restricting the options of those around them they restrict their own. By manipulating others, they bind themselves to limited relationships. People hope that in a manipulative relationship they will have total safety—they will be able to fully predict the other person's actions and the general course the relationship takes. In behaving this way, they think of the other person as an extension of themselves: If I will my arm to move, it will move. If I will my husband to be faithful, he will be faithful.

This is comforting but not realistic. People can never completely control anyone, not even themselves. So they live in fear that the other person will find the way out of their control, and to prevent this they control that person more and more tightly and become less and less content. Living in a world that is not controllable is frightening and chaotic. But as much as they may long to be in control, wise people know how to distinguish between what can be controlled and what cannot. The person one has the most control over is oneself. When control is a governing factor in one's life, paradoxical as this may seem, one is always dependent on others—looking to the outside world for support and legitimation, which leads to uncertainty and fear.

Contrast this dark and fear-ridden existence with the life of an autonomous person. Such people make decisions independently and take responsibility for them. If a decision turns out to be wrong, they acknowledge it: It doesn't destroy their self-image, and they are not overly concerned with other people's images of them. Autonomous individuals do not need to devise schemes to control others and can use their energies in more constructive ways.

Especially toward the beginning of therapy, the therapist is much more powerful than the client. The therapist interprets what the client says and does, but the client cannot do the same for the therapist nor even for himself/herself. This imbalance is what makes therapy work. The willingness to give up interpretative power to the therapist for a while allows the client to gradually learn how to accept more responsibility in real life. But the therapist's special power brings with it certain obligations: to be fair and nonexploitative, and *to be ready to give clients more power and responsibility as they become ready to assume it.*

Often clients enter therapy not only feeling helpless but even *wanting* to be helpless. They insist that the therapist tell them how to live and what to do: The therapist must be in control. Often, too, clients want the therapist to make them better through magic. These are ways of avoiding the issue of power—giving it up, refusing to take it. The therapist's job is to nudge the client, slowly and gradually, in the direction of autonomy: The client should lose the fear of being powerful or of being perceived as powerful. As time goes on, the therapist should seem to the client less and less "magical." Therapists should take steps to diminish the mystery, perhaps by talking about their lives or therapeutic methods to their clients, or by using humor to show that there is not an unbridgeable gulf between them. At the beginning, the therapist not only is actually more powerful than the client but is also perceived by the client as *immensely* more powerful; an important part of the therapist's work in each session is to lessen this imbalance a little and bring the relationship nearer to equality. The client's distorted view of both client and therapist is always the major issue in therapy, no matter what the content of the conversation at any time.

At the beginning of therapy, you will find it easiest to accept everything the therapist says without question, and you'll want the therapist to initiate almost everything. Later, however, if therapy is going well, the balance of power will shift. You will feel freer, gradually, to amend, enlarge upon, or contradict your therapist's interpretations, and the therapist should be willing to see you as becoming autonomous enough to do this successfully.

This means becoming your own therapist, acquiring many of the therapist's skills in order to work out your problems by yourself. For instance, in most forms of therapy, you spend a good deal of time talking about your dreams and the insight they give into the mind. At first, dream interpretation is mysterious—you really don't see how your therapist has made sense of your weird and murky recollections. But in time, you begin to learn; you keep track of recurrent patterns and notice significant changes in the structural or emotional content of your dreams; you see how the bizarre imagery makes allusion to the mundane details of your life. Your therapist should delight along with you in seeing you learn a new skill, even though it means you need the therapist a little less.

In the same way, early in therapy, when you feel distress, all you can do is pour out your pain to the therapist. At first, all you want is comfort, the assurance that someone is listening, someone cares. Then the therapist will link your reports of distress to events in the recent or distant past: Didn't this same kind of thing happen two months ago with your mother? Didn't you feel the same way about your boss? You find comfort now in being understood, in the knowledge that someone can make sense of your life: Your disasters aren't entirely random; there are reasons for them. Finally, you begin to see the recurrent patterns by yourself. Depression and anxiety don't descend inexplicably out of the blue. You still feel upset—but you know *why* a certain incident has caused such a lot of pain, and that very knowledge makes it less painful. After the first few months, your therapist should not tell you how you feel or why you feel that way; learning to be articulate about your feelings becomes your job. Your therapist's job is to let you do as much as you can by yourself as soon as you can, to take a less active role as soon as possible.

The therapist functions as a model of an autonomous human being—gives you a sense of what you'll be like at the end of therapy. At first, he/she does this by being explicit about his/her way of working and his/her reactions to what you say. This not only provides you with a gauge of the accuracy of your own impressions of other people's response to you, it also demonstrates comfortable and open communication within an individual's psyche and from person to person. The therapist thus models autonomous behavior, tacitly inviting you to try it. As therapy continues, you and your therapist should get closer and closer in your ability to communicate about yourselves. The therapist should not remain a godlike creature with unimaginable wisdom and powers. Part of the process is learning to see your therapist as another human being like yourself—and you are not ready to leave therapy until you feel this way. The therapist's powers diminish in your eyes as yours increase.

The personal relationship with your therapist is an important part of insight-oriented therapy. But perhaps the most intellectually exciting learning is found in the process of **interpretation.** As with so many aspects of therapy, interpretation is not unique to that setting. People interpret one another's words and actions, consciously or not. They figure out what something means, why people do what they do. But people are less accustomed to interpreting internally— making one part of their minds intelligible to another. This is what the interpetation of dreams is about, and this is what you learn to do in therapy.

To interpret is to clarify the meaning or intent of an unclear communication. The lack of clarity may stem from either of two sources: the speaker's inability or unwillingness to be clear, or the fact that speaker and hearer are using two different systems of communication. Speakers who have to say unpleasant things may purposely phrase them unclearly out of fear that others will react badly to the direct message. Sometimes people's thoughts are so threatening even to themselves that they set up a screen between the part of the mind that forms the intention to speak and the part that produces and understands the words, so that their real intentions remain hidden even from themselves. And finally, some people have one way of saying things, one way of mediating between what they want to express and the expression they choose, and others do it quite differently, though just as meaningfully. In therapy, people learn to recognize unclear communication and explore ways to change it. Interpretation alone makes sense of unclear communication and helps people to see the problems it creates. Interpretation is the first step toward better communication.

So interpretation is indispensable to insight-oriented therapy. But that should not obscure the fact that **unilateral interpretation** (the situation that exists in therapy in which the therapist can make interpretations of the client's behavior and not vice versa) entails an imbalance of power between the participants. To be able to interpret someone else's behavior is to make the implicit assumption that you understand that person better than he/she understands himself/herself. This is a position of great power.

So whoever is making unilateral interpretations has a monopoly on the power in a relationship. Yet we have said that psychotherapy should instill autonomy in the client. This can be accomplished only through shifts in the balance of power in the course of the therapeutic relationship, in part via changes in the manner and use of interpretation. The power of therapist and client will never be completely equal because the client, until the end of treatment, is receiving help and support from the therapist. The therapist should, session by session, give the client more and more of a role in the interpretative process. From the start, the client should have the right and the duty to question an interpretation that misses the mark—and this skepticism should be treated as reasonable doubt, not "resistance." Besides this, therapist and client should work toward **collaborative interpretation,** in which each is responsible for part of the structure: In an interpretation built on a metaphor, for instance, both should play a part in creating that met-aphor. Sharing the work of interpretation with the therapist, arguing for a position and being respected, gives the client a sense of autonomy that carries over from the therapist's office into the real world. The therapist could tell the client in words, again and again, about the importance of self-assertion and being responsible for one's own emotions; but until the client has had the experience of taking responsi-bility for his/her beliefs, the understanding of autonomy remains in the realm of the intellect. Taking an active part in the interpretative process is a sign of adulthood. Thera-pists who do not allow their clients this experience keep them in an infantile state. But a good interpretation, col-laboratively arrived at, augments the client's autonomy.

One client couldn't feel good about anything she did. After a few months of therapy, she told her therapist that she felt unable to do anything correctly.

THERAPIST: When did you start thinking of yourself this way?
CLIENT: I don't know. . . . But I just remembered that when-ever I wrapped a package, I would show it to my father, and invariably he would take it apart and rewrap it.
THERAPIST: How did that make you feel?
CLIENT: Like I never could do anything right. He was always correcting what I did.
THERAPIST: That must have been a very painful and per-vasive feeling. Maybe your father treated you as incompe-tent about other things, too. You always feel that someone has to rescue you by rewrapping your packages.

At this early point in the therapy, the interpretation is being made by the therapist alone. The client has the choice of accepting or rejecting it—that is, accepting or rejecting the metaphor of the inadequate package as symbolizing her lack of self-esteem—but if she accepts it, she doesn't add to it or embellish it with details that increase its personal meaning. Months later, however, she plays a more active role in the process.

CLIENT: My supervisor criticized me today, and I feel that all I do is mess up. I try so hard, but it's never good enough.
THERAPIST: Still can't wrap those packages, can you?
CLIENT: I guess I've always been a failure. It wasn't just the packages but everything I did that my father criticized.
THERAPIST: Maybe he is the only person on earth who can wrap packages properly. He seems to need to find fault with everything. Is your supervisor *only* critical?
CLIENT: Even though she criticized me, I just remembered that she also said I did something well last week. Maybe I have trouble remembering to put strings around my packages sometimes, but the paper is secure and the address is legible.

Checklists 6A and 6B will help you determine how well therapy is aiding you in achieving autonomy. The first examines your progress toward autonomy; the second, the extent to which your therapist is furthering it through the appropriate use of power.

Checklist 6A

YOUR PROGRESS TOWARD AUTONOMY

You are attaining autonomy if you:

1. feel less and less afraid of your therapist's (and other people's) judging you poorly.
2. find it easier to make decisions on your own.

3. can tell your therapist when he/she isn't on the right track.
4. can analyze your behavior on your own.
5. can see your therapist's minor faults without becoming unduly upset.
6. don't look to others to rescue you but take responsibility for your actions.
7. are more tolerant of other people and don't need total agreement.
8. find it easier than before to be by yourself and enjoy your own company.

Checklist 6B

YOUR THERAPIST'S USE OF POWER

Your therapist is using power appropriately if he/she:

1. is allowing you more and more opportunity to participate in the construction of interpretations.
2. is open to your corrections and criticism of interpretations.
3. refrains from giving you advice and encourages you to find your own solutions.
4. sometimes talks to you about his/her own experiences and feelings.
5. respects you and your judgment, and finds you a worthwhile person.
6. lets you handle difficult problems by yourself more and more.
7. is verbally supportive of your perspective on the world, at least sometimes.
8. is willing to change the rules when you give good reasons.

We have placed a great deal of stress on the therapist's willingness to relinquish power, on the grounds that only in this way can therapy do its work, *i.e.*, guide the client toward autonomy. But there is another, perhaps even more pressing, reason to require a lack of desire for power in a competent therapist: the great influence the therapist necessarily comes to exert over the client.

Psychotherapy developed in the nineteenth century out of hypnosis. Under hypnosis, a person is unusually susceptible to influence by the hypnotist: With certain exceptions, the subject will do what the hypnotist says to do, even things that will make the subject look ridiculous or things the subject normally cannot do. Hypnotists discovered that certain types of ailments, caused not by physical but by psychological processes, responded to the hypnotist's suggestion and vanished, even when the subject could not consciously will them away. From this beginning, early psychotherapists such as Freud learned that the therapist, like the hypnotist, can make patients or clients change attitudes or behaviors not under their conscious control purely through the strength of the therapist's personality as it is enhanced in the therapeutic setting. A client will sometimes get better only because the therapist wishes it, will take certain actions because the therapist has suggested— perhaps very subtly—that they would be met with approval.

This heightened suggestibility is an aspect of what is called, in technical therapeutic literature, the **transference.** Transference is an essential part of insight-oriented therapy. Different psychotherapeutic systems disagree on the extent of the transference that is normal, the forms it takes, how the therapist utilizes it, and what it means as a part of the client's symptoms, but all agree that it is always there.

Transference is the client's attributing to the therapist the attitudes or behaviors of significant people in the client's earlier life, especially parents. In classical psychoanalysis, the analyst is supposed to remain completely neutral so that any behavior the client attributes to him/her is presumed to result from the transference. Later, we will discuss the development and uses of transference in therapy. But here we want to concern ourselves with just one facet of it: the way in which the existence of the transference gives a therapist unusual power over the client.

The client's heightened suggestibility because of transference means that the therapist will have much more influence on a client's beliefs or behavior than anyone else in his/her adult life. This is a result of the client's unconscious perception of the therapist as a parental figure from early childhood: At that time in life, people normally are heavily influenced by their parents.

While transference, and its concomitant openness to suggestion, are an essential aspect of insight-oriented therapy and a potent force for change, like other potent remedies it may have dangerous side effects if incorrectly used. And if the therapist uses the power of the transference to induce the client to act for the therapist's advantage rather than the client's own, the therapist is acting in a highly untherapeutic and damaging way.

We would hope that someone who becomes a therapist has already learned enough about himself/herself not to need to take advantage of a client's suggestibility, but too many cases are known to the contrary for us to discount the possibility. When we spoke earlier of the dangers of extra-therapeutic contact between participants, we were alluding in part to these problems: Too often, the therapist is using such contacts for his/her own self-aggrandizement or even financial profit. Incredible as the latter may seem, just such a case has been reported in the newspapers. Because it is such a clear illustration of the dangers of incompetent therapy, we summarize it here.

Benson Ford, an heir of Henry Ford, had been in therapy over a number of years when his therapist began to make suggestions about financial investments—already a form of extra-therapeutic contact. Within a short time, the therapist had induced Ford to invest a great deal of money in a partnership between Ford and himself. Then the therapist surreptitiously removed much of Ford's investment to another company in which Ford had no interest. At the same time, the therapist apparently encouraged the alienation of Ford from his family (who presumably disapproved of the investment), and Ford brought a lawsuit against several family members.

Eventually Ford came to see the situation clearly, reconciled with his family, and sued the therapist. But the story stands as an unusually horrible example of a therapist's taking advantage of the therapeutic relationship.

To avoid an outcome like this, a client should be sure the therapist is not urging him/her into any extra-therapeutic encounters, for if these occur, the therapist's influence over the client will certainly impair the latter's judgment and put him/her at a disadvantage if the therapist intends anything unethical. And a therapist who encourages extra-therapeutic contacts is already a likely prospect for other forms of unethical behavior.

SUGGESTED READING

Freeman, Lucy, and Roy, Julie, *Betrayal*. New York, Pocket Books, 1977.

Haley, Jay, *Strategies of Psychotherapy*. New York, Grune and Stratton, 1963.

Watzlawick, Paul, *et al.*, *Pragmatics of Human Communication*. New York, Norton, 1967.

CHAPTER 7

Effective Therapy: Learning to Learn

A client's experience in therapy isn't entirely unique. The combination of assumptions and the context in which therapy occurs are probably different from all other experiences in life, but if you tease apart this combination of ingredients, you find that, one by one, each is an experience you've had before. Knowing this helps to demystify the process still further.

One familiar component is the *educational* aspect of therapy. We've all experienced education, of course. But we associate it with school, sitting with many others in class, listening to a teacher. And we probably think mostly of *facts* we learned by rote: Columbus discovered America in 1492, five times five is twenty-five, *i* before *e* except after *c*. After the memorization, there were tests, with right and wrong answers. By doing well on tests, students demonstrated that they had achieved mastery of the material and could put it aside, going on to something else.

On the surface, none of this sounds much like therapy as it has been described. So why do we say that therapy is a kind of education?

Clearly the setting is different: The client is alone, not a member of a class. And the method is different: The therapist doesn't tell the client facts but leads the client to new ways of thinking, feeling, and acting. What is learned in therapy is not factual information, or even techniques for arriving at this information, but a more complex, sophisticated, and unconscious process that has been called **learning to learn.**

Why do people need to embark on new forms of learning at the late stage in life at which they enter therapy? What is so special about the learning that goes on in therapy? To answer these questions, it will be useful to take a look at the various forms learning takes in people's lives.

We can talk about three levels of learning:

1. The rote learning of *facts*. When we learn in school that Columbus discovered America in 1492, that five times five is twenty-five, or that you put *i* before *e* except after *c*, these are examples of learning at this level. The information is useful for its own sake, but it doesn't lead anywhere or enable us to discover anything else.

2. The learning of *techniques* to discover facts. For instance, we learn how to put sounds together in order to read; to add one number to another, and the sum to another. This gives us more independence than does mere rote memorization: We become able to exert some control over our environment. This is another aspect of school learning.

3. The learning of learning, or *learning to learn*. This, too, happens in school, but we are less conscious of it—it isn't a separate, explicitly recognized subject like "reading" or "arithmetic," and while students are tested and graded on this aspect of learning, they usually don't realize it.

The ability to learn is built into a human being and is present from birth. A baby hears its parents talking and from this source of data, within a few years, fashions its own grammar and is able to utter sentences it has never before encountered. Rote memory, therefore, cannot account for this behavior. Nor can the child identify an explicit technique. Rather, the child has learned how to learn language—or perhaps has always unconsciously *known* how.

Learning to learn occurs outside therapy as well as in it. For instance, many people, when they begin to think about starting a family, are assailed by doubts of their competence to be parents. If the baby cries, will they know how to comfort it? Will they have the patience to go to it each time it cries? For many prospective parents, the anticipation is all the more stressful because they have never had a similar experience before—they have had no emotional training in parenting.

But suppose a new mother has, earlier in her life, raised a dog from puppyhood. Many—though certainly not all—of the stresses she will face with the new baby also occurred with the puppy. True, it isn't a human life. True, too, a puppy old enough to be taken from its mother is much less physically dependent than a human infant and requires much less of its caretakers both emotionally and physically. But there certainly are analogies. In both cases, one takes responsibility for a creature that cannot survive independently, with tremendous emotional and physical needs that must be met—not at the caretaker's convenience but as they arise. Both the infant and the puppy can make it clear, by crying, that they have needs but cannot make it clear what those needs are—a very anxiety-provoking circumstance for the caretaker.

By caring for a puppy, a person learns something about coping with its dependency, and his/her own anxieties arising from that dependency, in a relatively safe situation (at least, a vastly less frightening one than that of having a new baby!). The new owner learns how to care for the puppy: what its cries mean, which to act on, and which to ignore. Additionally though, he/she learns about learning to care for any dependent creature. The feeling of helplessness is gradually replaced by competence arising from knowing how to "translate" the puppy's cries and act appropriately.

When a baby arrives, the new mother will of course become quickly aware that caring for the baby isn't like caring for the puppy. But she brings a sense of competence and self-confidence from the earlier experience to the new one. She understands that just as she once learned how to care for the puppy, in the same way she will be able to learn to care for the baby. What she brings to the later experience is her ability to learn.

In theory, then, people come into the world already knowing how to learn—some kinds of things. In school, they extend that repertoire. They learn, for instance, how to pay attention; how to select out of a lecture, or a book, the salient points; how to reproduce the crucial steps in a proof or a logical argument. Their education, if it is adequate, teaches them how to learn *intellectual* data by invoking skills they were born with.

People are also born with the knowledge of how to learn emotional information: how to recognize love (and other emotions), how to give it and receive it. But just as people can sometimes receive intellectual misinformation in school (such as learning that George Washington chopped down a cherry tree), so they can get emotional misinformation at home. And the falsehoods people "learn" early in life about their emotions and needs and how to get them satisfied become fixed in their minds, a part of their characters. They aren't aware of having learned them (any more than they remember having learned language—it's a part of them). For example, suppose that in your parents' home, no one ever knocked before entering someone else's room—privacy was not much valued. Now you're living with a group of house-mates. When you enter their rooms without knocking, you feel their coldness and are afraid they don't like you. But the actual problem is that the "rule" you learned from your parents is different from the one your housemates are fol-lowing. They expect you to be following their rule. It isn't that their rule is better but just that there are more of them than there are of you. If you want things to go smoothly, you'll have to substitute their rule for yours.

The misinformation learned in childhood eventually causes trouble: The world becomes unpredictable and dangerous. No one else seems to be playing according to the old rules, which therefore no longer produce good results. At this point, perhaps, people may try to use the kind of explicit techniques they learned in school. They behave the same way in every situation. Or they make up rules to predict, and thereby control, their environment—as though the world worked like multiplication tables. But this solution gen-erally leads to frustration: The world keeps playing unex-pected variations of the game, and people continually feel baffled. It is this bafflement, this sense of being up against a concrete wall, that brings people into therapy: Many kinds of therapy refer to this repetitive, unsatisfactory behavior as **neurosis.** In therapy, the unconscious knowledge people have of how to learn—which has, in large measure, been dormant since early childhood—is re-awakened and made conscious, so that they learn how to reinterpret their environment and respond to changes in it intelligently. It is not so much that in therapy people gain an entirely new skill but that they recover an old one. Since that kind of learning was last active when they were dependent, therapy must re-create a modified dependency; because they were then powerless, it must place them again in a position of relative powerlessness.

It would be wonderful if we all had earlier relevant positive experiences to refer back to in new emotional experiences. But too many early crises were dealt with unsatisfactorily, so that people learned the wrong things, and as a result, they encounter new experiences with feelings of helplessness, incompetence, lack of control, and barely concealed panic. So people have to acquire the good emotional experience in an artificial way—that is, in therapy.

Part of therapy is learning to learn, becoming able to extract from earlier experiences the insight needed to solve current problems. In order to do this, clients have to acquire new ways of looking at themselves and their prior experiences. This is a never-ending process of learning to look for deeper emotional responses and understanding the pattern that they form.

Learning—in therapy and outside—often feels risky because it threatens apparently well-ordered lives with chaos. By forcing people to confront both current and older feelings and experiences that had been kept safely buried out of conscious awareness, therapy often initially provokes a sense of being overwhelmed. The client may feel things are getting worse, not better, and may doubt that the risks of insight are worth the promised reward—which now seems vague and very far off. A good therapist, by being encouraging and supportive, will make this difficult time easier for the client and will push the client to insights only as fast as the client can endure—but will not stop the work or provide false reassurance. In time, the client will see how everything fits together and will understand that the pain and chaos were necessary precursors of the pleasure of self-knowledge. Then, seeing how pain is worth enduring in the "unreal" world of therapy, the client can begin to expose himself/herself to the risks necessary for growth and change in "real" life, confident that there, too, the payoff will be worth the risk.

If earlier experiences were frightening or painful, people may have distorted or misperceived reality in order to cope with them. In the future, when partially similar situations arise, they see them from the same perspective. Although as adults they are now strong enough to cope directly with unpleasant reality, they still retreat to their old misperceptions and do not notice the important differences between the old and new situations. They respond by reflex, unthinkingly, rather than by intelligently analyzing the situation to determine the most appropriate course of action. Therapy teaches the client to overcome the fear aroused by the original situation, enough to be able to perceive the new event as unique and respond to it appropriately.

Like any kind of learning, good therapy is both painful and exhilarating. One would think there is enough pain in life without planning for it and even paying money to arrange it. Why does therapy have to be painful? The pain of therapy is the pain of breaking out of the old and familiar, of seeing oneself and one's world in a new way, perhaps from a less flattering or comforting angle. It's a little like exercise: If you go at it vigorously, your muscles will probably ache for a day or two afterward, because you have forced them to do what they haven't done before. But after the initial pain, the body is stronger, more limber and flexible—it has learned to adapt to new patterns, to allow more possibility of movement. The body feels better, more vibrant and energetic. In the same way, psychotherapy makes the mind stretch at the cost of some pain at the start. But as long as there is guidance, as long as therapist and client know why the pain is there and how much is tolerable at each stage of therapy, the eventual benefits will far outweigh temporary discomfort.

Often people who have undergone a great deal of suffering in earlier life have learned **defenses**—ways of postponing or hiding the distress. If one can confront pain directly, and learn from it, one is much less apt to repeat painful experiences. But since defenses involve the suppression of all kinds of feelings—pleasure as well as pain—they diminish the enjoyment of life, making it dull and monotonous. And worse: In avoiding possible bad experiences, one never really solves the conflicts underlying them. So they are apt to recur throughout life. By breaking through the defenses, experiencing the pain (which is seldom as bad in reality as in imagination), one can see clearly what the source of the difficulty is and either banish it entirely or (more likely) bring it down to manageable proportions. Learning itself is painful, because it brings one into contact with the original troubling experience as well as the difficulty of changing persistent ways of seeing and deep behavior patterns. It involves unlearning the old and familiar, which was at least safe in being predictable. The new is always somewhat frightening or threatening, because we don't know what to expect.

The most difficult point for the client comes when, having recognized the unsatisfactoriness of old patterns, he/she feels sorrow and disgust at being caught up in them but doesn't yet see clearly how they can be changed, or sees how to change but is not yet able to act. The client feels like a student in a class who doesn't understand the subject matter: The tests keep coming back full of red pencil marks, but the student doesn't see how to do better—only that he/she is a failure. But in time, with diligence and courage, and perhaps a clear explanation from the teacher, the student sees the point, begins to make progress, and starts looking forward to the class.

The pain of therapy is balanced by exhilaration from several sources. For one thing, the client for the first time is making sense to somebody and is therefore no longer totally isolated or crazy or inarticulate. Somebody cares enough to listen closely to what he/she says and to remember it from session to session. Secondly, it's exciting to begin to understand where one's fears come from: They don't arise out of nowhere but out of earlier experiences. By understanding them and their history, one can take the first step in controlling them. Someone who has always felt at the mercy of unpredictable emotions will find it exhilarating to begin to gain control over them.

Finally, pain and exhilaration work together in therapy. As the therapist explains the origins of the painful feelings, their intensity is diminished. Seeing old fears dissipate is exhilarating. Becoming able to do things that were formerly impossible is thrilling. None of these—change, pain, exhilaration—is possible without the others, and therapy induces the client to endure the difficult parts to get to the rewarding ones.

One of the most difficult aspects of the therapeutic process is learning to take risks. Because this is such an important feature of therapy, the therapist does not regularly dispense advice or instructions. The risks clients confront in therapy are not physical or financial—getting run over crossing against the light or losing money in the stock market—but psychological. In their fear of the psychological consequences of an action (rejection, shame, abandonment, guilt, and so forth), people may become unable to act at all or may avoid responsibility for the outcome by manipulating another person into doing what is perceived as risky. But there is no life without risk: It cannot and should not be avoided. Rather, it should be experienced and used as a tool for learning. Running a psychological risk, because it has both intellectual and emotional effects, is the best way to learn. In fact, *there is no true learning without risk*, and therapy gives people the strength to experience both.

We are not encouraging uncontrolled risk-taking in real life. One thing to be learned in therapy is the difference between risks that *are* and *are not* worth taking. Often someone who is terrified of one kind of risk will go to great lengths in running risks of other kinds that serve no valid function but deflect the risk-taker's attention from the real one. So, for instance, a person hesitating to confront a spouse may take to reckless driving. But in therapy, risk-taking is subjected to client's and therapist's scrutiny. In this controlled situation, taking modified risks is encouraged, and the actual experience of the risky situation is explored: The competent therapist will "milk" the situation for all its meanings for the client and will refer to similar previous patterns. With the client's feelings accessible to discussion, earlier situations that gave rise to current feelings can be explored.

Learning to learn, then, is a cornerstone of the therapeutic process. Therapy does not exist without it. Because learning involves placing oneself in new situations, or seeing familiar situations in new ways, and the unfamiliar is frightening, good therapy exposes a client to risk. While risk itself is not necessarily valuable, and may be dangerous, the controlled psychological risks of therapy are beneficial, and surmounting them provides a first experience of autonomy and control over one's life.

Learning can also be frightening because it threatens well-ordered lives with chaos. When people learn something new, their previously well-arranged conceptions of how everything fits together are taken apart. But eventually the new information comes to fit together, and people achieve a sense of mastery and order, creating exhilaration. In the same way, therapy, which makes people rethink their current and their earlier feelings, can create a sense of chaos and disorder. Eventually, after coming to terms with the feeling of chaos, people feel exhilarated at gaining a sense of control over their destiny. And finally, the bridge from chaos to confidence in therapy gives clients a model for the same kind of change elsewhere in their lives.

SUGGESTED READING

Bateson, Gregory, *Steps to an Ecology of Mind.* New York, Ballantine, 1972.

CHAPTER 8

Some Myths About Therapy

Part of learning to learn is becoming able to tolerate and resolve contradiction. The therapeutic experience itself presents several such contradictions, resolvable through deeper understanding. For example, people often believe that they have to select a therapist of a particular kind: a therapist who concentrates on the past and the unconscious *or* a therapist who explores the client's present life. But it is a myth that therapy must be of one kind or another. What people find when they have been in productive therapy for a while is that the past and the present *cannot* be separated, that understanding of each enriches the other. In this way, what is learned about the therapeutic process carries over to the rest of life, because what often seem to be all-or-nothing situations are resolved much more satisfactorily when people realize that there are many ways of understanding them. So the apparently rigorous distinctions among types of therapy and even aspects of the therapeutic process that seem opposed to each other are all parts of an indivisible whole. In this chapter, we discuss five contradictions commonly encountered in therapy.

First of all, therapy has an *intrapsychic* as well as an *interpersonal* focus. The therapist helps clients look not only at the way they perceive events and people from their childhood (the intrapsychic aspect) but also at current relationships and concerns (the interpersonal aspect), and helps clients bring the two together.

One woman, a thirty-year-old successful lawyer, had a boyfriend who continually criticized the way she dressed. Rather than ignore or counter the criticism, she would start to cry. Her therapist asked why she needed the man's approval.

"Why shouldn't I feel devastated?" asked the client. "He's awfully important to me."

"Of course. Everyone is hurt when someone they care about criticizes them," said the therapist, "but to break down crying each time is excessive. Where does the extra feeling come from, I wonder?"

Even though intellectually the client appreciated the therapist's point, the crying went on. She couldn't help feeling worthless and despondent when attacked. Her professional success didn't give her enough self-esteem to push criticisms aside. Then, during one session, the client was talking about how her father had been critical of almost everything about her from her childhood on. "It used to make me feel horrible," she said. "Each time it happened I would go to my room and cry."

Her therapist asked, "Is that the same way you feel when you're criticized now?"

If the therapist had concentrated merely on the client's current behavior, and had looked only at her feelings toward people currently in her life, the client never would have understood *why* she reacted as she did. The need to cry at criticism would have continued to seem to her like some extraneous imposition by forces outside her control: "The devil made me do it." And because outside forces apparently brought it on, it would have made no sense to her to take the responsibility for stopping it. But once she saw how, when she was younger and more helpless, she had herself developed the crying response to mitigate her father's harshness, she could see that she herself had devised this way of acting and had allowed it to become a part of her even now, when it no longer did her any good. So she could take steps to change the way she handled criticism. Looking at the present alone, like looking at the past alone, would not have given this client the complete understanding necessary to make the change.

Another myth is that therapy must be either directive or non-directive. In fact, therapy is directive and non-directive at once. In directive therapy, a therapist gives a client specific advice about life and frequently assigns "homework"— tasks to do between appointments that will connect the feelings and responses uncovered in sessions with real-life events, focusing the client's attention sharply on his/her responses. Especially at the beginning, the therapist can provide a sense of order and connection through reasonable suggestions about how to get out of predicaments. Homework often makes clearer to the client how to apply what is discovered in the therapy sessions to real life. Homework can also help the client in crisis to manage anxiety between sessions, when the therapist is unavailable. In non-directive therapy, the therapist plays a much less active role: listening, interpreting, connecting the client's remarks, but neither initiating topics of discussion nor telling the client what to do outside therapy. In strongly non-directive therapy, such as classical psychoanalysis, the therapist will not make suggestions of any kind, even if the client asks for them: That would interfere with the process of **free association** (the client's commitment to say anything that comes to mind without trying to organize it).

Non-directive therapists argue first that directiveness may keep a client dependent, second that it may prevent the client from following his/her own train of thought to important but hidden material. But like other valid techniques, non-directiveness can be carried too far. For that matter, so can its opposite. The beginning client, who sees the therapist as a figure of wisdom and authority, may wonder why the therapist should not give advice. Part of learning to learn is gaining the confidence to find one's own solutions. Dependency fostered by advice-giving is not a step toward autonomy. A client who can depend on the therapist for directions will never learn true self-reliance. Also, the idea that the therapist is always there to give advice suggests to an insecure client that the therapist, like the omniscient parent of one's infancy, knows best. Therapy should encourage realistic perceptions, not foster the same old fantasies. On the other hand, sometimes a client will ramble on without focusing hour after hour, without communicating much that is meaningful. A direct question or comment from the therapist may help such a client to be clearer and more to the point, making each session more valuable.

One such client had talked for several sessions about selling his car and buying a new one. He would go over and over the pros and cons and what kind of new car to buy. He was just as indecisive about changing apartments, getting a new typewriter, leaving school, and so on. Talking about the issues didn't seem to help clarify the client's choices or to make it clear why decisions were so difficult for him. After two sessions devoted to the relative advantages of a Honda versus a Toyota, the therapist suggested that he flip a coin, as he seemed to have no real basis on which to make a decision—but pay close attention to his feelings as he did so. While the client still found the decision agonizing, at least in the next session he was able to talk about his internal process of deciding and how it made him feel, rather than focusing on external issues, and he realized that his inability to reach a decision was related to his fear of doing anything that would bring him pleasure, as he felt he didn't deserve it.

Most therapeutic sessions are not purely "directive" or "non-directive." In a typical session, there will be moments when the client is encouraged to explore whatever comes to mind, without prompting from the therapist; others when the therapist, seeing in the client's unfocused statements a connection between issues, will bring them together with a question or statement. Or the therapist may point out two separate issues in a story the client relates, which the client sees as the same.

A client, a freelance writer, told her therapist about her lunch with a magazine editor. The editor had rejected her manuscript, and the client had suggested they meet in the hope that the editor would offer suggestions to improve her work. But the editor sat there saying very little. The client found herself chattering away, feeling unable to stop—a failure both socially and professionally. Her therapist said: "There are really two issues here. One has to do with how you handled your anxiety by talking too much, the second with the fact that although the editor wasn't very competent—after all, it is an editor's job to provide constructive criticism—you let her make *you* feel inadequate." The client's telling her story at length was non-directive, but the therapist directed her toward seeing something about herself and the way she dealt with anxiety.

We have said that therapy, unlike ordinary friendship, is not *reciprocal:* The participants have distinct and non-interchangeable roles. Nevertheless, it is a myth that a relationship is purely reciprocal or purely non-reciprocal: All therapy involves *some* **reciprocity.** Part of the client's job is to learn to participate in reciprocal relationships, of which therapy should provide a partial model. Although the roles of client and therapist are distinct, the therapist should be confident and human enough to allow, when it is therapeutically desirable, some behavior in the direction of greater equality—for instance, the acknowledgment of mistakes, the acceptance of compliments and perhaps symbolic gifts, the admission of personal bias where relevant, and the disclosure of personal information in the service of the therapy. (See the discussion of these issues in the next chapter.) All of these actions bring the therapist closer to the client, as a vulnerable human being with feelings and needs, not the mere dispenser of a service or a godlike figure with no human frailties. A therapist with some opinions and weaknesses seems more real and three-dimensional and less of an idealization. Moreover, as the therapist in fact *is* a human being with biases, if he/she cannot openly acknowledge this, the client will sense soon enough the therapist's insecurity and will lose confidence in him/her. So, paradoxically, by becoming more vulnerable the therapist becomes more secure.

Because clients reveal a great deal about themselves in therapy, the therapist may seem to be acting strangely by refraining from most forms of self-disclosure. The client may feel uncomfortable in this non-reciprocal situation, but therapists have their reasons for behaving this way. Some therapists consider it dangerous or untherapeutic to reveal anything personal to the client: It would discourage the client from having and expressing fantasies about the therapist. But the client will still create many revealing fantasies to explore. It is practically impossible to stop their development entirely. But the therapist's willingness to make personal revelations—as long as they are in the service of the therapy and not for the therapist's own comfort or self-aggrandizement—can be valuable. Implicit in the therapist's disclosures is the message that the therapist, too, has had problems and conflicts but has overcome them with insight, humor, and action. In this way, therapist and client can share in the knowledge that both are flawed but neither irretrievably so.

Risk and safety are two more apparent opposites that must occur together in therapy to bring about change. We talked earlier about the necessity for risk in therapy as in life, to foster growth. But everyone is aware of the dangers of uncontrolled risk. Therapy allows risk under supervision—a "safe risk," like walking a tightrope with a safety net.

Three kinds of risk occur in therapy. One is **interpersonal risk:** It involves self-revelation and possible loss of face or the threat of rejection by the therapist—for example, as a result of revealing that you have stolen money from a friend. The second is **intrapsychic risk,** the danger of confronting irrational fears previously hidden and suddenly unavoidable. It is always a risk to re-experience deep fears—to remember situations that were painful and unresolved. Frequently people want to run away, fearing that the feelings will be overwhelming or endless. Re-experiencing your fears in the presence of the therapist is a continual process of risk-taking. But the fact that the therapist is there, listening and caring, mitigates the risk, creating a feeling of safety. Clients who are not continually running risks within the therapeutic framework are not really in therapy—they will not use the process as a tool for growth.

The third is **situational risk:** The client is testing the proffered reliability of the therapist and the strength of the therapeutic relationship. Situational risk is important because it revives some of the strongest anxieties of childhood: Will my parents be there when I need them? Can I trust them to protect and support me? The client tends to test the situational risk in therapy by questioning small things: Does the therapist keep appointments? Can the therapist remember—and be discreet about—information supplied by the client? The risk to the client is the threat of finding out that this hope of trustworthiness, too, is illusory. But if, time after time, or at least the overwhelming majority of times, the therapist proves reliable, the client can learn that the world is a less perilous place than he/she thought.

From the start of therapy, one client was continually testing whether his therapist deserved his trust. At the beginning of each session, he would bring up questions about what the therapist had said the session before. His comments revealed that he had spent a good deal of time ruminating over the therapist's remarks so as to find the least positive interpretation of them. The therapist explained her remarks and wondered why, although the client had understood them while he was in her office, afterward he seemed to need to go over them and pick them apart. It seemed important to him to question the therapist's good intentions. She pointed out: "It seems that you want me to jump through hoops for you to prove that I am trustworthy. I am willing to do this for as long as you need, but let's talk about why you are able to trust me when you're here, but as soon as you leave, you have to undo that trust." The next week, the client reported that he realized one of the reasons he had trouble trusting his therapist was that his mother frequently concealed criticism in seemingly positive statements. So he could never believe a positive statement, and he found it necessary to be one jump ahead of anyone important to him.

When all these risks have been encountered in a climate of benevolence, and surmounted, change becomes increasingly likely. Change is most apt to occur when a person feels comfortable but not completely so.

A final apparent contradiction is that between the real and the **fantasy** elements in the therapeutic relationship. The last chapter discussed transference, clients' endowing their therapists with characteristics of significant people from the past. But there is more than fantasy to the therapeutic relationship. And in fact, even transference is not totally fantasy: The therapist's real personality and behavior contribute to its development. Through the transference, the client sees the therapist in different ways at various stages of the therapy: at one point, perhaps, as the all-giving mother hoped for early in childhood; at another, the withdrawing and punitive father remembered from adolescence. By repeating these emotional experiences, the client gives the therapist a view into his/her mind. By having the distortions of the transference repeatedly pointed out by the therapist, the client begins to understand that many current real-world relationships are being based unrealistically on patterns retained from the past.

The therapist's impression of the client is also partially based on earlier experiences and unresolved needs—reactions referred to as **countertransference.** A therapist who is an oldest child may see clients as younger siblings, needing guidance but rather annoying, although nothing in the clients' actual characters or behavior suggests this. Or a client inclined to self-pity might arouse in a therapist the unpleasant

recollection of a self-pitying mother, generating dispropor-
tionate irritation in the therapist.

Therapist and client also share a real relationship. Even
though the therapist conceals some thoughts, feelings, and
way of life from the client, much can be ascertained by the
interested client—every client finds speculations about the
therapist irresistible. (In all relationships, after all, much is
not shared: No one knows *everything* about even the most
intimate friends.) Among the most important things shared
in the therapeutic relationship is an intimacy based on caring and interest: Both participants want to understand the
client. Also, the risks of therapy for the client bind the two
closer, as happens with two people who share any dangerous
venture. And, too, part of this "real" aspect are the kinds
of responsible behavior expected in all mature relationships
on the part of both participants: to keep appointments and
other commitments, and to do the therapeutic work. Both
judge each other in part through the same questions people
ask about friends and acquaintances: Is the client/therapist
prompt? Is he/she willing to work to keep the relationship
alive? Does he/she have a sense of humor?

It is useful to think of the emotional work of therapy in
terms of Diagram I. The fantasy relationships—transference
on the client's part, countertransference on the therapist's—
each occupy one-fifth of the work of therapy; the client's
practicing of new attitudes and behavior, one-fifth; and the
real human relationship between the two people in the room,
the remainder.

Reality and *fantasy* also balance each other. What people
"recall" from their childhood is a mixture of accurate memories of events that really happened; distorted memories of
actual events, in which the way things happened, or the
reason why they happened, is altered; and fantasies, that is,
outright fabrications. It is the client's job to report to the

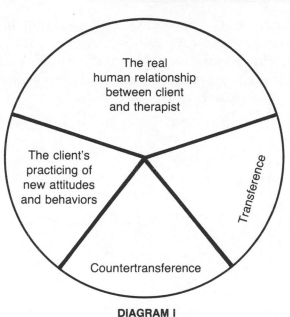

DIAGRAM I
THE EMOTIONAL WORK OF THERAPY

therapist all memories, and the therapist's to determine which reports represent reality, which fantasy, and which a mixture. The therapist finds all of these "recollections" equally valid and important in the therapeutic process: To prove that a "memory" represents an event that could not have taken place does not make the client a liar or a crazy person, nor does it make that "memory" useless. Rather, it is the business of therapist and client together to figure out *why* the client has fabricated the fantasy and what function it serves in the client's past and present mental life. Incidentally, although it is generally agreed by therapists that some "memories" represent reality more accurately than others, it is the responsibility of a compassionate and involved therapist to give the client the benefit of the doubt: A memory should be presumed true until conclusively proven otherwise, not the reverse.

The combination of apparent opposites is therefore a necessary part of therapy. By learning to understand and tolerate, and finally resolve, these contradictions, the client becomes more competent to assess the confusions present everywhere in reality.

CHAPTER 9

Shifting the Balance of Power

All the special assumptions, relationships, and forms of communication that compose psychotherapy work to one end: the development of a client's autonomy. Paradoxically, a client becomes more autonomous by yielding power to the therapist for the period of therapy. Eventually, if the therapy is to be effective, the power balance must shift to become more egalitarian, although never completely so. Forms of therapy in which the initial imbalance remains till the end are necessarily less effective in developing autonomy than those in which a gradual shift occurs.

The therapist's job, therefore, is to work with the client to make gradual changes in the balance of power through a number of techniques. For instance, the therapist can use incidents from his/her own life as illustrations of how to confront problems, or at least not be overwhelmed by them. This makes the relationship more reciprocal by diminishing the gap in power and authority between the participants. The therapist emerges as someone who, like the client, must wrestle with real difficulties in life. Then, because the therapist is engaging in self-disclosure along with the client, the therapeutic relationship itself begins to approach the equality of true friendship. The therapist can begin to make these disclosures as soon as the client becomes able to deal comfortably with them—not getting upset at being forced to perceive the therapist as less than perfect and not being in an overwhelming state of crisis. We are not advocating that the therapist take up the client's hour with personal problems: The technique must be carefully controlled if it is to be therapeutic for the client rather than the therapist. The example must be directly relevant to the client's narrative and needs, and the therapist should stress the solution above the problem. Finally, the vignette should be short and to the point: It should not distract the client from the telling of his/her own story.

A client was talking about how her husband never missed an opportunity to criticize her. She responded to his criticism with arguments defending herself. Since they never convinced him to change his mind, she would get increasingly upset. Her therapist said: "That reminds me of the time my mother was visiting me some years ago. I was six months pregnant at the time. My mother said, 'I never realized how good my marriage was until I saw what kind of man your husband was.'"

The client asked: "What did you do?"

"I said, laughing, 'Mom, what should I do? Pack my bags and leave and look for a new husband—now, when I'm six months pregnant?'" The therapist was showing the client that humor was much more effective than argument in combating criticism.

The therapist could have said the same thing in the form of direct advice: "Why not just make a joke?" But an autobiographical disclosure bolsters the client's self-esteem as direct advice does not, by reminding the client that the therapist also has had problems to solve and that he/she trusts the client enough to admit this; the client can see that even his/her seemingly insurmountable present problems have solutions, as the therapist can look back and laugh at what must have been a terrible moment. Expressing such ideas indirectly lets clients figure things out for themselves rather than having them explained, as parents do for children. Figuring out the point of stories also gives clients a chance to develop independent ideas and perhaps gain an understanding of different people's different conversational (and other) strategies.

Humor is important in the therapeutic process, allowing therapist and client to make jokes and laugh together. Humor is important everywhere in life, but especially in therapy, where serious and frightening topics often arise. Humor is a way to confront difficult truths from a safe distance, remaining involved yet maintaining a perspective. The therapist can show the client how to use humor outside the therapy as well, to take the sting out of touchy situations. Then, too, for therapist and client, engaged as they are in painful work that builds tension between them, laughing together at a joke brings them closer, creating an intimacy that helps resolve feelings of hurt and resentment.

Sometimes the client, rather than the therapist, will want to do something to change the power imbalance, often by giving gifts. People give gifts for a variety of reasons, some of which are more obvious to them than others. A present can be given simply out of affection or appreciation or a desire to surprise and delight someone. But a gift can also carry a hidden price tag: It can be a bribe or an attempt to appear more powerful than the recipient. After all, to give a gift creates, in the recipient, a sense of obligation, a feeling that the giver is owed something. Or giving a gift may be an attempt to establish, or claim, intimacy. Or, finally, it can be an attempt (probably unconscious) to get "better treatment" from the therapist out of gratitude: more time, or more respect, or leniency in payment of bills, or more favorable interpretations. So it is natural that at times a client will feel strongly impelled to give the therapist a gift, which may be material (a book, a bottle of wine, or a tip on the stock market), a product of the client's own creativity (a painting or poem), or more symbolically a statement of how much therapy means to the client. You need not agonize beforehand over your motives (although it doesn't hurt to give some consideration to the matter), but you should be aware of the multiplicity of reasons clients have for wanting to give gifts in therapy. You should not feel rejected or insulted if the therapist insists on examining the motives behind your gift, or even refuses it. This is one way in which therapy is *not* like friendship. Depending on the nature of the gift itself and its symbolic meaning, the therapist may choose to accept it or not and examine the reasons behind it or not.

The therapist, too, may give the client gifts—usually of a different kind and always carefully considered. Often they are *symbolic*, indications that the therapist really cares for and understands the client at times in the therapy when the client needs to be reminded of this: expressions of sorrow at a loss, praise at a triumph, acknowledgment that the client has been working especially hard in therapy. The therapist may also suggest or lend books that would be therapeutically useful to the client. To give gifts of either kind to a client is a way of saying, indirectly, "I am interested in you and care about what you're doing." To say this explicitly might sound demeaning or hypocritical. But to say it symbolically makes it easier to understand and believe. It is also more emotionally powerful because it exposes the giver to risk: It could be rejected. But it makes the relationship more solid if it is accepted.

A client and his therapist had, over a long period, pieced together from vague recollections and unclear clues likely events of the client's childhood that seemed to help him understand his current problems. Later, he remarked to his therapist: "My older brother was in town this weekend, and I talked to him about our family. He remembered, on his own, many of the events that you and I had reconstructed. The fact that he corroborated our conclusions made me realize again how valuable the therapy is to me and how much I can trust your judgment." The client didn't really need to report this to the therapist. More than mere corroboration of the therapist's ideas, the story was intended to convey the client's appreciation for the therapy: It was intended as a gift, one which the therapist had no trouble accepting with appreciation.

Another client was having difficulty writing her novel, because she was embarrassed about its more sensual passages. She was afraid that the experiences she was trying to put into the book (and relate to her therapist), many autobiographical, were too strange for anyone to understand. Instead of trying to reassure her directly, the therapist suggested she read Colette or Anaïs Nin's erotica and lent them to her.

The client's need to take risks is obvious, but the therapist, too, must run risks to be truly a part of the process and to illustrate for the client that such dangers are an inevitable and surmountable part of life. Besides, the therapist's willingness to face the same discomforts as the client makes the relationship more equal. Then, too, taking risks keeps therapist and client alert and interested, and the keen involvement on both their parts makes therapy vital and exciting. The therapist runs two kinds of risks, one arising intrinsically out of the therapeutic process itself, the other introduced intentionally by the therapist. The process of making interpretations itself is risky, because the interpretation can be wrong. As much of a therapist's authority is derived from correct interpretations, a wrong interpretation is apt to make the therapist look incompetent, at least temporarily. It is useful for the client to bear a few things in mind, for the times when interpretations will miss the mark. First, it is highly likely that even the best therapist's interpretations will sometimes not be useful for the client: The therapist would have to be a fortune-teller to achieve one-hundred-percent accuracy. Second, it makes less sense to speak of "right" and "wrong" interpretations than those that are "helpful" or "unhelpful." Even an interpretation that is "wrong" in not representing the client's actual psychic reality may, nonetheless, be useful in suggesting new areas to explore—or even just because the effort shows the therapist cares and is hard at work.

Actually, an interpretation is seldom *altogether* right or wrong—in part, it's the client's job to winnow the wheat from the chaff, taking only what is useful. The therapist, recognizing the uncertainties of the process, should be careful to present interpretations not as truths from Mount Sinai but as tentative speculations for the client to confirm or reject. The therapist might begin, "I have a hunch . . ." or, "A possible association just struck me . . ." rather than, say, "This is what that dream means." The client should "try on" the interpretation, keeping the parts that work and discarding the rest. What the client should understand from any interpretation is that the therapist is dedicated to the client and committed to the therapeutic work. And in some respects, a partially correct interpretation may have more therapeutic value than one that is perfectly right. Correcting a partially right interpretation is a way for the client to learn responsibility and practice assertiveness, as well as an experience of collaboration for both participants. (Of course, the therapist's interpretations should be right much more often than they are wrong.)

The second kind of therapeutic risk undertaken by the therapist is experimentation with the power imbalance. Despite its hazards, the potential gain is great. Being allowed to exercise more and more power over time gives clients an increased sense of competence and shows them how much the therapist is willing to risk to make the therapy work.

A client had continual severe problems discovering and expressing her needs and wishes. After a long period analyzing this problem without making much progress, the therapist decided that the only way to break through the client's fear of risk was to take a real and unorthodox risk himself. He bet a session's fee that the client could make a list of three goals she wanted for her life. A stipulation on the bet was that once the client had named these goals, she would have to work on achieving them.

The next week she came to the session with her list. The therapist's gamble had so impressed her that she felt more deeply committed to the therapy, more willing to reveal herself, more competent and adventurous.

Therapy has been called "dead serious play." It is "play"— a game—insofar as the relationship between client and therapist is not "real" and the expectations of ordinary life about what is important, what is truthful, what is mentionable, are subject to a different, special set of rules not unlike, say, the rules of chess. Hence therapy can be seen as a kind of allusive statement about the rest of life, referring to it, a part of it, but not at the same level.

Therapy talks about things that are intangible and abstract —hard to understand. We can see how our bodies work (in some ways, anyway), but we cannot see our minds at work. Additionally, much of what a therapist has to say to a client is apt to be painful to hear. Often, difficult communications are made easier if they are indirect—so that the hearer has to take a moment or two to understand them.

For these reasons, allusive language is and always has been very important in therapy. Writing for one another, as well as talking to clients, therapists tend to couch their ideas in allusion and indirect expression. Typically, the symbols therapists choose to convey their ideas to clients are unilaterally developed: The client is the passive recipient, like the reader of a poem. But it is better if the metaphors are jointly developed rather than being created and controlled by therapists alone, and they should seem valid to both participants from every perspective. By participating actively in the creation of metaphor, the client gains a sense of control over both the therapy and his/her life, since the metaphor gives it new meaning. And because client and therapist are creating the metaphor together, both risk its failure and share the opportunity to succeed in the process of creation. So the joint making of metaphors brings client and therapist closer together in several ways.

Allusive language is common in all types of therapy, but in more traditional types, it is the therapist who is exclusively responsible for its creation. Additionally, more often than not, rather than fresh and living metaphors devised specifically for particular clients' needs, the therapist brings out hackneyed proverbs and stale clichés: "Where there's smoke there's fire," "You can't make an omelet without cracking eggs." While these sayings can be useful for impressing on clients the universality of their situations, they have a distancing, if not trivializing, emotional effect. The client feels forced into a pre-existing mold, not perceived as a unique individual. Citing "universally true" proverbs is a way for the therapist to reinforce his/her authority: If everyone has always seen things this way, the therapist can't be wrong. Hence these devices are favored by authoritarian parents, and clients may resent them for good reason.

Metaphors created jointly by therapist and client feel very different. Rather than closing off the client's options, defining only some responses as "normal," shared metaphors open up possibilities, new ways of looking at things. One client, a clothes designer, was having difficulties with her long-standing boyfriend. She saw him as an authority, brighter and more competent than she in every way. Yet she was a talented, successful, and personable woman. In a session in which she was rhapsodizing about the boyfriend, her therapist said her relationship with him was like her relationship to her design business: In both she took unpromising raw materials and made something wonderful of them. "Except," said the client, "at work I get to sign my name to what I create."

A therapist who is sincere in the desire to move toward greater equality in the therapeutic relationship will be careful to give full respect to the client's perceptions, even when they are different from the therapist's own. Even when the client disagrees with an interpretation that the therapist feels completely sure of, the therapist should listen to the client's point of view. In therapy, as in other aspects of life, no one has a monopoly on the truth. If therapy is to serve as a model of a good relationship, the therapist should not set up as an ideal an authoritarian personality who cannot tolerate disagreement. Also, disparate as the two viewpoints may seem at first, there may be a way to reconcile them. Tolerance on the therapist's part is especially important, because new clients in therapy, like beginners in any field, are often overly critical of their own work. A therapist who is tolerant and accepting of clients' ventures into self-examination is building their self-esteem, enabling them to deal with what is unknown and confusing in life. Also, it helps clients to develop their interpretative skills so that when it is time to leave therapy, they are able to interpret for themselves.

This willingness to remain open to the client's point of view is especially important in dream interpretation. If therapist and client disagree on the meaning of an event or symbol in a dream, the client's understanding is nearly always right. A therapist who is unable to yield to the client in this is a therapist to beware of. (This doesn't mean that the therapist should not offer interpretations, and even press the client at times to see if they have validity. But the therapist should be willing to yield if the client insists.)

All of these techniques are invaluable because:

1. they model for the client ways of dealing with difficulties in real life;
2. they teach the client how to build and continue egalitarian relationships;
3. they help the client develop responsibility for feelings and actions;
4. they foster warmth and intimacy between client and therapist.

Therefore it is important that at least some of them be typical of your therapeutic experience.

After about six months of therapy, you should be able to examine your therapy dispassionately to see if it is working as it should.

Checklist 9

YOUR THERAPY AFTER SIX MONTHS

1. Sometimes you come to therapy with a particular problem to work on, and sometimes you're willing to just let things come up.
2. You think about your therapist as a three-dimensional person rather than an idealized authority or dispenser of services.
3. Although you report your experiences to your therapist and depend on his/her guidance for interpreting their full significance, you are able to understand their meaning at least partially on your own.
*4. Certain events from your past have been identified by yourself and your therapist as important.
5. You can maintain an interpretation of a dream or an event different from that of your therapist.
*6. You see a relationship between events in your current life and your past.
*7. Even when you can't control your behavior, you can tell when you've been acting irrationally.
*8. The world looks less black-and-white, less fearful, and less chaotic; more hopeful and more open to possibility.

SCORING: If you have not answered *all* the starred (*) items positively, your therapy is not doing its job. You should begin to think of finding another therapist. Trying to negotiate these questions with your therapist is probably beside the point. You should cut your losses and go. For the others, if you can't answer positively, some discussion with the therapist is in order, so that both of you can decide where there are problems and what to do about them.

CHAPTER 10

Communication in Psychotherapy

Therapeutic communication sounds like ordinary conversation in many ways but is different from it. It is like ordinary conversation on the surface: The participants take turns talking to each other. They each make statements and ask questions. Each has to interpret what the other person says. There may be interruptions and silences that, as in ordinary conversation, make the participants feel a little uncomfortable. The participants may make jokes and may sometimes misunderstand each other.

These apparent similarities may make people starting in therapy overlook, or misunderstand, the very real and significant differences between therapeutic and ordinary conversation. One of the first things a person entering therapy must learn is a set of new rules for communication. But it is less the surface appearances that must change than the deeper intentions for which utterances are used. To give an example, while both client and therapist can ask each other questions, questions *function* differently for each of them. The therapist may ask the client, "Are you upset about something today?" and expect a complete response, treating the question as nothing more or less than a question requiring an answer. But suppose the client asks the same question of the therapist. Typically, the therapist will not reply with the answer the client wanted. Rather, he/she may say, "Why is it important for you to know?" To the client, this sort of response may seem rejecting and cold, as indeed it would be in an ordinary conversation with a friend. But the client quickly learns that the response, like the question that precipitated it, has a different meaning in therapy—in fact, any of several meanings. One of the therapist's jobs is to determine just what a client's question means. The question might represent the client's deeper concern, perhaps a worry that the therapist is angry with him/her. Or perhaps it is the first sign that the client sees the therapist as a real person, not just as the fantasy figure of the beginning of therapy. Or asking a question might indicate the client's desire to become one with the therapist by knowing as much as possible about him/her. It is important for the therapist to understand what the question means, which the therapist can do only by treating the question as a statement about the client's needs—not a true request for information.

Sometimes the therapist must confront a client directly, by saying something that would be considered intrusive in ordinary conversation with a friend. After two years of therapy, one client was becoming more assertive with the people in her life, especially her mother. Her mother had agreed to send her money to buy clothes for Christmas, and the client had agreed to tell her mother what she had bought. Then a parcel of clothes arrived from her mother, all too small and unflattering in style. In her therapy hour, the client discussed confronting her mother about her actions. The therapist asked what questions she wanted to ask. The client had trouble formulating a question but finally said: "Mom, I want to know why you sent me that package of clothes."

Her therapist countered: "Is that the question you *really* want to ask? . . . My hunch is that you are less interested in the clothes than in the fact that once again, your mother has shown that she can't be trusted."

The client said, "But why would she do a thing like that?" She found it much more compelling to think about her mother's motivations than to experience her deeper feelings of anger and disillusionment about her mother's untrustworthiness. The more her therapist led her back to the latter issue, the more painful it was for the client to think about it.

Finally the therapist said, "Your mother has let you down again and again in the same way, but you protect yourself against recognizing that by trying to figure out individual motives for each occasion. And you do this not only with your mother but with everyone important in your life."

The client finally recognized her tendency to get sidetracked by figuring out other people's motivations instead of identifying her own needs. The therapist directly contradicted and confronted the client in a way that would be insulting or hurtful in ordinary conversation, where we tend to leave it up to other people, at least outwardly, to account for their behavior, and avoid open inquiry into their motives. But the therapist, in the service of growth, has to bring the client's blind spots into sharp focus.

People learn to use language as children. At that time, they learn not only words and the rules for putting them together but also how to hold conversations properly—how to begin and end, how to take turns, and how to understand what other people need to know. When they are grown up, people assume that they know all they need to know about their own language, that there is nothing left to learn. But entering therapy is like visiting a foreign country: One has to learn a new language if one wants to derive full benefit from the trip. Because therapy in this country is usually conducted in English, the fact that a new client must learn a new mode of communication is not obvious. But it is true—not so much because the surface *forms* of the communication are different (they really aren't) but because the purposes for which things are said by therapist and client are different. Therefore the meanings of things that are said the same way may be different, and conventional utterances that are understood one way in ordinary conversation may have a different meaning or function in a therapeutic conversation. Moreover, therapy often works via **paradox,** by making a client confront two statements or situations that cannot both be true at once but are. The antitheses we talked about in Chapter 9 are examples of therapeutic paradoxes. In ordinary conversation, our ideal is to be clear and unambiguous. Paradoxical statements are not appreciated. Learning to understand, tolerate, use, and perhaps, finally, enjoy paradox is the very heart of therapy. By learning to appreciate paradoxical forms of language, the client learns in part how to change and how to tolerate change. A skilled therapist can guide a client through the pain and confusion and make the special communication of psychotherapy both intellectually and emotionally exhilarating. And although the special conditions and forms of therapeutic conversation can sometimes be stressful and difficult (for client and therapist alike), other aspects of the process are extraordinarily warm and loving—far beyond the communication of ordinary friendship.

The therapist, then, has to talk to the client in ways that are special. The client, too, must learn a new way to talk. In outside life, some people are open and direct, some reserved, and everyone is more open with some people than with others. But in therapy, clients must always try to be open and direct to the best of their abilities. In other relationships, people censor what they say before they say it: Perhaps it will hurt the other person or be damaging to the speaker, or it is beside the point or nonsensical or bizarre. In therapy, the rule is to "say whatever comes to mind," without imposing any order or censorship on it. Of course, this is an impossible ideal: Quite often you will find yourself hesitating, or be unable to say something, or be able to say it only in a roundabout way. Your therapist will be able to see when you're more hesitant, or more unclear, than usual, and will assume that you are finding something hard to say directly. So it's important to try to be as open as possible, for that attitude encourages exploration and discovery. But it's natural to encounter difficulties in this area; these difficulties are themselves essential to the therapeutic process.

It may seem to you, at first, that all your therapist has to do is listen to you. In a sense, this is true—but just as you learn to speak in therapy in a way that is different from the way you speak to others in your life, your therapist's listening is not the same as a friend's. It has been called "evenly suspended attention," a kind of relaxed attentiveness. It is listening not for the expression of particular ideas but for the gradual emergence of a pattern.

During a session, a good therapist is not passively taking in what the client has to say but is working very hard. Your therapist is thinking about the overt and hidden meanings of everything you say and determining which topics require confrontation, elaboration, or encouragement. As you speak, your therapist is remembering other things you have talked about—dreams, past relationships, early life—and putting them together with new information to form a cohesive but constantly changing picture of your psyche. Your therapist is listening for clues about who you are and how you see yourself. These clues become apparent from hidden connections in the surface content of what you are saying. You may have brought up a topic feeling it was totally unrelated to anything else, but your therapist's sensitive ear will pick up nuances suggesting an unconscious connection. Having this pointed out to you can be the first step toward understanding why you keep doing the same irrational things again and again—even when you know better.

For example, the way you approach relationships with the opposite sex and your feelings about your work might seem totally unrelated. You *know*, let's say, that you find it hard to make commitments in a relationship. Perhaps you also have noticed that you are good at starting writing projects but always lose enthusiasm halfway through. To you, these are unrelated pieces of a jigsaw puzzle. Your therapist, however, listening to you talk about both (in different sessions), detects a repetition of a word, a phrase, a feeling. For instance, asked to imagine full involvement in both, you talk about them both in the same way: You'd be "responsible" for someone, for something. And your therapist, from this clue, will discern the importance of "responsibility" in both aspects of your life and trace your uneasiness back to its origin. Two pieces of the puzzle interlock, and you can suddenly make out a pattern. It's not solved yet—there is still a lot to do—but at least you're no longer totally in the dark.

Your therapist is listening, too, for *how* you say things, for example, whether you say, "I am very depressed," in a flat, dead tone or histrionically: How do you see your depression? Are you using it to make yourself seem interesting or to give your life some drama? Or do you view the depression as beyond your control, something that has taken over your mind? Your therapist also pays attention to whether your conversation is interesting or boring, in both content and style: Do you vary your voice and use compelling images and vivid descriptions, or tell your story in a monotone, with repetitive words? If the therapist is bored, perhaps you are bored as well. Any story told by a storyteller whose emotions are fully engaged is interesting. Why can't you get involved in your own story? In any case, you're building a barrier between you and the therapist, trying to create emotional distance: Being boring can be defensive.

In other words, while people in ordinary conversation listen (consciously, at any rate) primarily to the *content* of what others are saying, the therapist is at least as interested in the form itself. The therapist is also listening for connections in your communication, similarities of form that link apparently disparate topics. You might have a favorite turn of phrase that you repeat, seemingly for no reason, but upon investigation, you may find it has hidden meaning for you. Or your overall style of communication can give the therapist a picture of how your mind works. You might use a lot of passive sentences, saying, for instance, "The dishes got broken," when you actually mean, "I broke the dishes." The therapist might point out that the use of passives is a distancing device—it separates speakers from their feelings and from their hearers. Or the frequent use of sentences in which the speaker is acted upon rather than being the actor (*e.g.*, "She got me to marry her" or "People are always out to get me") could indicate that the speaker feels helpless and a victim of circumstances. Or, by casting statements in the form of questions, a person might show indecisiveness and unwillingness to make a commitment, linguistic or otherwise. Or a speaker's use of questions might indicate an unusual degree of concern with the opinions or approval of others. Because a particular style of speaking might have any of several interpretations, the therapist must consider what has been discovered about the client's behavior and attitudes. A good therapist will point out not only preferences for certain forms of expression but also the possible deeper meaning of those preferences. The therapist is looking for repeated patterns that form a picture of the way you imagine the world and your relationship to it. So linguistic patterns provide your therapist with evidence of how your mind works and also give the therapist concrete examples by which to prove it to you. The therapist cannot very easily demonstrate your behavior to you but can show you patterns in the way you talk, patterns of which you yourself were previously unaware.

Therapists also use language to model better communication for clients to emulate. People entering therapy are often not accustomed to making their feelings appropriately and effectively explicit in words. The problem usually isn't that clients cannot talk about feelings at all; more often, they will be able to talk volubly but will use words that avoid, rather than capture, the painful feelings: clichés, generalizations, or jargon rather than the precise and simple word that would make things immediately clear. This sort of talk is fine for superficial conversation in which people don't want to expose themselves too deeply, but it is of no use in therapy, where the aim is to learn to understand feelings. To help clients get a sense of the difference between words that precisely convey feelings and empty expressions, a therapist could present "translations" like these from the vague word or cliché to the meaningful expression:

1. "She was weird to me." = "She wouldn't talk to me and made me feel rejected."
2. "I have a problem with my superego." = "I will steal anything that isn't tied down."
3. "I thought she was nice." = "I hope she has sex with me."
4. "My child is going through a difficult stage." = "I would like to bat that little bastard's head against the wall."
5. "He seemed to think I was okay." = "He complimented all my achievements and made me feel very special."

These examples show why people disappear behind meaningless words. First, it's easier to have pat phrases that can be trotted out for a wide variety of occasions than to have to search for the precise word to describe each. Then, by being vague, people can avoid facing difficulties and conflicts head-on. Third, imprecise communication allows people to present their best face to others, to acknowledge their imperfections without admitting how serious they are and invite others to give them the benefit of the doubt. Although in ordinary conversation these strategies have their virtues, they are anti-therapeutic. Not only do they make the therapist's work of unraveling the meaning of the client's communication much harder, but by postponing or preventing the client's confrontation with serious issues, they build up the latter's fears rather than dispelling them, as open discussion would do. While you will find yourself at times irresistibly drawn to empty expression in therapeutic sessions, it is to be hoped that your therapist will discover and point out to you the significance of your doing so, and that, as a result, your use of such language as well as your need for it will diminish in time.

The therapist's encouragement of clear and precise language has two other purposes as well. First, it makes it easier for the therapist to understand the client. The way the client tells the story of a specific event should be like the way a good novelist leads a reader into a novel: The clearer and more explicit the details about setting and characters, the more the reader can perceive the intention of the novelist and be drawn into the plot. Then, too, the client learns from becoming able to talk more clearly. At first, even the *idea* of thinking certain thoughts is too painful or uncomfortable. The fuzzy language is a screen to hide behind. But being forced to come out from behind the screen shows the client that facing unpleasant reality directly is not necessarily lethal, and moreover, it's the only way to begin to change that reality.

As we have said that clarity and precision are of paramount importance for the client, it will seem puzzling when we say that for the therapist, these are not always virtues. Often, it is best for the therapist to communicate indirectly or not completely clearly—for instance, by using hedges. **Hedges** are words speakers use to blunt the meaning, or expressive power, of what they are saying. Therefore hedges tend to occur in people's speech under two circumstances: one, to qualify a claim that would otherwise be too strong, and two, when they feel powerless or feel that they should present themselves as powerless or unassertive, leaving it up to the other person to decide what the communication is really about. We can get an idea of these different functions by observing two examples of the use of the hedge *sorta* (more conventionally expressed in written form as *sort of*):

1. John is sorta tall.
2. That was sorta dumb of you.

The first would most naturally be used in the first situation above. The speaker is asserting that while John is reasonably tall, others are taller—his tallness is qualified, not absolute. In the second case, though, an interpretation of this kind makes less sense. We don't rate "dumb behavior" on a quantified scale as we do tallness. The second sentence really means something like, "That was very dumb of you, but I don't want to offend you by saying it directly, so I'll just tone it down a bit."

Besides *sorta,* many other hedges exist. Some words are sometimes hedges, but not always. Starting a sentence with *I think, I guess,* or *It seems to me* is often a hedge, as is phrasing a declarative (*You feel uncomfortable.*) as a question (*Do you feel uncomfortable?*). The modal auxiliaries *can, may, must,* and *should* often are used to hedge the force of sentences in which they occur. The use of passive sentences can likewise mitigate the force of assertions.

People often see hedges as "weasel words"—ways of making statements without taking full responsibility for them, leaving the burden of understanding up to others, not taking the trouble to clarify ideas before expressing them, etc. So sometimes people in power (for instance, parents and teachers) criticize the use of hedges. ("I wish you wouldn't say *y'know* in every sentence!") The irony is that very often, hedges are used out of a feeling of powerlessness, inadequacy, and inferiority. The more users are criticized, the more they will feel compelled to use hedges.

In therapy, then, the *client's* use of hedges is often self-protective and therefore deserving of scrutiny (but *kind* scrutiny). But the *therapist's* hedges are for another, though related, purpose and are legitimate: The therapist, in using hedges to qualify and weaken the strength of assertions (especially those that entail "speaking for" a client, telling the client what's going on in his/her mind), is helping to diminish his/her authority and power relative to the client's, as well as avoiding intolerable intrusiveness. In making interpretations, for instance, there is a danger of overwhelming the client and making it impossible for the client to disagree. By hedging the interpretation, for example, by saying, "My hunch is . . ." or, "Could it be that . . . ," the therapist is giving the client some power to determine the validity of the interpretation without battering the client's self-esteem or risking an open confrontation.

Because the building and preservation of the client's self-esteem are such important tasks, the therapist, in saying things to the client that might be painful, often must be careful to couch those comments in hedged or indirect language. To hear difficult ideas this way gives clients room within which to understand them and a way of taking them in and making them their own rather than having them imposed by someone else. The therapist doles out the "bitter medicine" in small doses that the client can swallow at his/her own pace. This way the client feels some control over the treatment rather than having it force-fed—which both is coercive and takes the responsibility for it out of the client's hands.

Clients enter and remain in therapy to deal with problems. They are therefore in a state of weakness relative to the therapist—a position not likely to foster self-esteem. Yet self-esteem is crucial: It provides the strength to view oneself in a less-than-favorable light. The client must always feel, no matter how harshly the therapist is seeing him/her, that the therapist regards him/her as a person capable of change and worthy of respect. Only a person who consciously acknowledges these qualities in himself/herself is able to change. Therefore the therapist must constantly balance the client's need to be confronted with the need for self-esteem.

A client should be able to talk about anything without being made to feel worthless, stupid, crazy, or immoral. The therapist should not suggest in any way that something the client confides should not have been said or is too awful to discuss. Therapists are generally aware of the many dangers of judgmental statements and seek to avoid them, but they can fall unwittingly into them in indirect form. A therapist who would be careful to avoid direct suggestions like, "Of course you should get a job. A man is supposed to support his family," may without realizing it impart the same message to the client by saying, "Most men in this culture have jobs. It makes them feel good and allows people to respect them." In some ways, the latter statement is even more dangerous than the former: The indirectness may suggest to the client that the point is totally obvious and beyond argument, while one could take issue with a direct statement. Often just the veiled suggestion that the therapist finds the client's ideas or behavior unacceptable will close off honest discussion and make the therapy useless.

The client should be on the alert for judgmental statements phrased as rules that are true for all time. If you think your therapist is using statements of this kind, bring it up. Some examples are:

1. A mother belongs with her children.
2. Sex with many partners is unhealthy.
3. Relationships between older women and younger men never work out.

4. If teenagers have sex, it will ruin their lives.
5. It is unfair to run risks if there are people who depend on you.
6. Children are happiest when their mother is at home with them.

While language is of great importance in therapy, of equal importance is what is *not* said, or what is communicated without words. Silence, it has been remarked, is eloquent. Just as a word can mean any of several things, so can a silence, on both the therapist's and the client's part.

For the client, the therapist's silence may be difficult to deal with. In ordinary conversation, silence from the other participant is very often negative: It signifies a lack of interest or disapproval. So a client, having spoken and received no response, may well feel that something is wrong. This may be correct. Perhaps the therapist feels disapproval too profound to express in words. But more often, silence means that the therapist wants to give the client more time to reflect on what has been said. For the therapist to speak at that moment would be to discourage the flow of ideas and associations. A therapist's silence could also signal a profound sense of "togetherness" with the client, an empathy so deep that nothing need be said. But the therapist should indicate this in some way, probably non-verbally; the client should not be left alone, isolated and afraid.

A client's silence also has several possible meanings. The client may be so overwhelmed by what has been discussed that he/she has nothing to say for a while; the client may be overcome by emotion or confused by conflicting ideas. Or he/she may have "spaced out" defensively—that is, become temporarily unable to think coherently and express ideas intelligibly, a way of avoiding the ideas or emotions that have surged up. Or he/she may be trying to express a negative emotion in a way that will not lose the therapist's love and approval. Or the client may be angry—because the therapist is forcing him/her to confront something painful, or because the therapist was late in beginning the session, or because the therapist seems not to be listening or reminds the client suddenly of the mother the client didn't like—and, as punishment, is withholding the "gift" of speech from the therapist. Silence, then, can be giving or withholding, warm or cold, and can express a range of emotions from empathy to fury. If you find yourself falling silent for long stretches (which is bound to happen at some point in your therapy), it will be useful to remark on the silence to your therapist; together, you can figure out what kind of silence it is and the probable reasons for it.

One client often fell into long silences during the therapeutic hour, and her therapist eventually commented on this fact: "I notice that you are silent for a large part of every therapy hour. How does your silence feel?"

The client said: "Sometimes it is pleasant—I am remembering good things from my life. At other times, I feel lost and frightened."

Her therapist said: "Try to let me know which kind of silence you are experiencing. If you like, I could help you with the silences you find uncomfortable, both here and outside therapy."

The client learned to indicate which silences were oppressive, and the therapist became able to direct her attention to discovering the reason for the silence, often by having her report her thoughts during it. This helped diminish her unproductive rumination, in therapy and outside it.

Words and silence are not people's only means of communication. There is also non-verbal (**extralinguistic** and

paralinguistic) communication. Extralinguistic communication involves gestures, eye movements, stance, posture, and other bodily signals. Intentionally or (more often) not, people communicate in these ways, and other people understand what is meant even if they are not aware of how they came by their understanding. A therapist should be as alert to a client's non-verbal communication as to the verbal and should use it as the basis for interpretations. Especially meaningful are discrepancies between verbal and non-verbal signs, which suggest unconscious conflicts within the client. For instance, a client described a new job as exciting and promising, but at the same time, he slumped in his chair and spoke in a monotone, staring at the floor. The therapist pointed this out, asking the client which—words or actions—expressed his real feeling.

In addition, non-verbal communication involves *paralinguistic* messages—what is expressed in the voice but not in the words themselves: intonation, pitch, variation, and speed of speech. These are often clues to emotion, and like the non-verbal message, can be at odds with the intentional, verbal message. So a client might describe her marriage as calm and comfortable in a tense, worried voice, and the therapist would detect a double message and comment on it. The discovery and interpretation of extralinguistic and paralinguistic messages, as well as their verification by the client, are much more difficult than the interpretation of the verbal message. Moreover, these cannot be fully understood until some time after therapy has begun: A baseline must be established for the client's normal posture and voice, for instance, in order to know when something is unusual and worthy of comment. All of this demands special skill and subtlety on the part of the therapist, both to detect anomalies and to prove them tactfully but unambiguously to the client. But it is an invaluable part of the process, illustrating as it does when done right the complexity of emotions and needs that make up the human psyche and the depth of unconscious needs, wishes, and fears.

In this chapter, we have been discussing the use in therapy of communication to discuss communication—or **meta-communication.** Therapy uses communication of all kinds—verbal and nonverbal, speech and silence, intentional and unintentional, intellectual and emotional—to deepen understanding and create change. Studying how someone communicates is a way of getting to understand how that person thinks. The way clients talk becomes as useful for understanding them as what they talk about. Metacommunication is difficult at first for both therapist and client to learn—it is different from what is normal or permissible elsewhere. Normally, people don't metacommunicate if they can help it, because it seems intrusive. But in therapy, people must learn to inspect the deeper parts of themselves, and language is the route by which to do this. Clients and therapists have to learn to use language not only as a vehicle by which to intentionally express ideas and needs but also as a diagnostic tool and an instrument of cure: Language tells people things about themselves that had not been apparent, and through talking about those things, people can gain some control over them and, eventually, change them.

In therapy, then, the client gradually becomes more and more skillful in communicating and in understanding communication, partly through the therapist's example, partly because there is less need to hide things from himself/herself. By learning to be open with the therapist in words, the client becomes able to be open and trusting with other people elsewhere in life. A client who is encouraged, through the therapist's insistence on direct language, to face truths in a way that can maintain and augment self-esteem will ultimately be able to live a freer life, with more choices and more satisfaction. Language alone does not create reality, but it can be the first reality that one is capable of changing.

Part Three

THE END AND BEYOND

CHAPTER 11

Ending the Therapy

You've been in therapy for a while, and it feels very comfortable. Some of the problems that brought you into therapy have gone away, and your life is running much more smoothly. Now you begin to wonder how much longer it will be useful to continue in therapy.

You've noticed that your feelings about the sessions are changing. Earlier in your therapy, you couldn't wait for each session. Sometimes you even got there early because there was so much you wanted to say. Fifty minutes was never long enough. Now you find it hard to get there on time, and when you're there, you're not sure how to fill up the hour. Sometimes you feel as if you're repeating stories only to fill up time. You seem to be getting less out of each session: Have you reached the point of diminishing returns?

A lessening of the urgency and a turning from concern with your psyche to a greater involvement with the outside world are indications that therapy is close to fulfilling its purpose. But these feelings usually aren't distinct and unambiguous. Is there any way to tell when you have accomplished all that you can in therapy? Is there a length of time beyond which therapy should not continue? Everyone knows about people for whom therapy became virtually lifelong—ten or twenty years, or even more. It seems clear that prolonging the therapeutic process like this is not apt to be productive. But how do you know when it's been going on too long?

At first, the thought of termination makes you feel anxious. As long as you're in therapy, you feel that you are accomplishing things, that you're facing your problems and trying hard to get better. Once you're on your own, will you continue to improve? Or will you lose the ground you have so painfully gained? These are serious concerns, but you should remember that gaining insight—the work of the therapeutic sessions themselves—is only half the job. You need to practice what you have learned until it becomes a part of you. Only when you are totally on your own can you be fully competent in managing your life. As long as you have to look to your therapist for confirmation of your competence, you are not autonomous.

You may worry, too, that once you have left your therapist, all your half-resolved problems will become worse and you will find yourself as helpless as you were when you started. While in all probability this will not happen, you should realize that the decision to terminate is not irrevocable. There is nothing shameful about re-entering therapy. Rather, think of therapy as a lifelong process: A major part of the work is done in collaboration with a therapist, but much is achieved outside formal therapy as well. Also, changes in your life may lead you to consider returning to therapy: having a child, a death in the family, or divorce. So terminating does not necessarily mean ending the therapeutic process forever.

Readiness for termination cannot be measured in months or years. It depends in part on the shape you were in when you entered therapy and in part on what you hoped to accomplish. It also depends on your therapist's expertise—some therapists achieve results more quickly than others—and on your therapist's ability to let you go. Some therapists (who may be excellent in other ways) become dependent on their clients, not only financially but also emotionally. Like a mother who cannot let her children go as they grow older, such a therapist is threatened by a client's growth and is reluctant to acknowledge a client's readiness to be independent. These therapists—and they are by no means uncommon—will be unable to help a client realize it's time to go. So you may have to figure this out for yourself.

There are other reasons that a therapist may be reluctant to broach termination of therapy when a client is ready. The therapist may fear that the client will (incorrectly) take the suggestion as a rejection or a statement of despair: "I'm giving up on you." Like other people, a therapist is uncomfortable about creating negative situations and therefore may not want to be the first one to mention termination.

Also, it can be counter-therapeutic for a therapist to suggest termination, because therapy has as a principal goal the development of autonomy. Autonomy includes the ability to evaluate oneself accurately, to make personal decisions on the basis of that evaluation, and to act promptly and firmly on those decisions, even when the action might create difficulties in important relationships. The decision to terminate therapy, along with the ability to discuss it dispassionately, plan for it sensibly, and act on it, is an excellent test of a client's autonomy. A client who can do these things has proved his/her readiness for termination; one who relies on the therapist to do the job has not. So it's important for the therapist to let the client play the major role in the process of termination—though it is not inappropriate for a therapist to drop hints, now and then, that a client is approaching the time for termination.

When a client leaves, the therapist has as much to lose as to gain. There is a loss in income, and perhaps a loss in self-esteem because he/she is no longer needed. And, especially after lengthy therapy, the therapist can become as emotionally attached to the client as the client is to the therapist and may have difficulty severing the connection. Depending on the therapist's strength and resources, these factors may lead a therapist to hang on to a client longer than is healthy.

On the positive side, the most obvious gain to the therapist when a client ends therapy is that of seeing someone grow and knowing that one has made a difference in someone's life, like a parent seeing a child become independent. If the gain is to outweigh the loss, the therapist must feel both personally and professionally secure, so that the client is not used to gratify the therapist's own needs. If you feel uneasy about abandoning a therapist who has given you so much and seems reluctant to let you go, remember that as a client, you must do what is right for you: When you feel it's time for you to leave therapy, you should leave, with or without your therapist's blessings.

If you are having some of the feelings described in this chapter, it may be time for you to determine whether you are ready to leave. The answer is never easy or obvious. Checklist 11 will give you some guidelines to help you make up your mind, and you can use your answers as a basis of discussion with your therapist.

Checklist 11

ARE YOU READY TO TERMINATE?

1. You have a pretty good sense of what's going on in your life and why.
2. Even when things go wrong, you feel you can cope.
3. Irrational emotion doesn't dominate your life.
4. You are not sabotaging yourself as you used to.
5. You are usually satisfied with the quality of your relationships.
6. You feel hopeful a good deal of the time.
7. Your fantasy life is generally optimistic.
8. You can imagine life without your therapist.
9. You have some tools to deal with your moments of irrationality.
10. You can cry without shame.
11. You less frequently feel the need to withdraw or isolate yourself defensively.
12. You find it easier to see the good points in other people and in yourself.
13. You feel a desire to be on your own.

SCORING: If you can answer "yes" to more than nine of the above items, you are ready to plan the termination of your therapy.

Termination should not be abrupt but should be discussed and planned with your therapist. You can plan to terminate in, say, a month, or three months or more, but you will want to schedule some sessions in which to explore your feelings about termination and your future life. Sometimes, in a moment of anger (justified or otherwise), a client will break off therapy abruptly, in a single session and without prior warning. Such a gesture almost always causes later regrets. As with any separation from someone important, termination is best accomplished gradually and rationally. It is important to differentiate between the gradual process of termination agreed upon by both participants at the successful conclusion of therapy and the abrupt breaking off of therapy for the kinds of reasons discussed in earlier chapters, as a result of serious flaws in the therapy. We are advocating a gradual process only in the former case, though even in the latter, the decision to end therapy should be communicated to the therapist in person.

In your discussion of termination with your therapist, be sure to explore the possibility of returning—which will be easiest, of course, if you are leaving with your therapist's blessings. If the therapist is unhappy or resentful at your departure, leave-taking may well be both final and abrupt.

You may wonder how you will be able to cope with the return of any symptoms, what you would do in a real crisis, and whether your therapist will take you back into therapy if it becomes necessary. These questions are ambiguous. On the one hand, they may mean, "Am I healthy enough to be on my own?", on the other, "Will the therapist still be there for me if I can't manage by myself?" During the sessions before termination, your therapist should guide you through imaginary situations that are potentially distressing, and you should try to devise ways to cope with them. Of course, all possibilities cannot be imagined, and imagination is different from reality. Therefore you may want to leave open the option of getting in touch with your therapist in a future crisis.

There are several ways to make termination as painless as possible. One is to withdraw from therapy gradually: If you've been seeing your therapist once a week, taper it off to twice a month, then once a month. Or you can take a "sabbatical"—stop therapy for a pre-arranged period, perhaps six months. Even if you have not made previous arrangements for returning, you should be able to assume that if, in the future, the need for more therapy arises, you can return for as long as you need.

Once termination is under active discussion, a client can expect to feel ambivalent. On the positive side is a new sense of independence as well as more free time and money. On the other side is the loss of the therapist's support and the end of an important relationship. Besides, at the time of termination, the client must finally recognize that he/she cannot be completely "cured"—life is much more satisfactory than it was but not totally perfect. While therapy was ongoing, the client could enjoy imagining a perfect post-therapy future. Now, facing termination, the client must see this for what it is—a fantasy.

As the agreed-upon time approaches, you will find yourself asking some questions: How can I tell if I am "well"? Can I function without my therapist? If you have scored nine or better on Checklist 11, these questions do not represent a real concern.

Before therapy comes to an end, client and therapist should clearly and openly discuss the nature of their future relationship. This can range from having no contact whatsoever, to occasional phone conversations, to true friendship. If your therapist seems reluctant to establish a post-therapeutic relationship, don't jump to the conclusion that he/she doesn't like you. Many therapists have for valid reasons established a strict policy against friendship with former clients. You should also ask yourself what sort of relationship you are envisioning: a truly egalitarian friendship or a relationship in which the therapist continues to be seen as all-wise and all-giving and the client as a needy child. A therapist may be understandably wary of such unrewarding entanglements and may discourage continuing relations with *all* clients because of experiences of this kind in the past. You should also remember that wanting to leave open the possibility of returning to therapy with this therapist and entering into a friendship with him/her are mutually exclusive. And as good therapists are harder to find than friends, it would be wise to confine your interaction with this person to therapy alone.

Although anxieties and crises will continue to arise after therapy is over, the ex-client can use the tools gained in therapy to continue the therapeutic work indefinitely and confront these problems in a productive way. The learning to learn that constitutes good therapy is applicable to the rest of life. The therapeutic situation ends, but therapeutic thinking continues.

CHAPTER 12

Being Your Own Therapist

Y ou've been out of therapy for a while. For some time, things have gone reasonably well: Minor crises came up, but you handled them competently, and you felt that you had things well under control. But now new problems are arising, or some of the old ones are returning: They weren't solved as completely as you had thought. You think about re-entering therapy. Sometimes this is the appropriate thing to do. But often, people feel reluctant to undertake this large commitment again. Is there an alternative—a way to use what you learned in therapy without having to go through the whole procedure again?

Or maybe, after reading this far, you feel you'd really profit from therapy. But for various practical reasons, it's impossible for you—at least at present. Perhaps you've tried to find a therapist you could work comfortably with but could find no one who gave you a feeling of trust. Or you are financially (or emotionally) dependent on someone else (say you're an adolescent or a wife without access to funds of your own), and that person is unwilling or unable to support your therapy, and public agencies aren't available to you. Or, finally, perhaps, you feel drawn to the idea of therapy, but your friends and family are strongly against the idea: Nobody in their experience sees a therapist unless they're "crazy," and you're not willing to identify yourself publicly in this way and face everyone's ridicule. Is there any way you can derive at least some of the benefits of therapy without seeing a therapist?

While there is no complete substitute for good therapy, a dedicated and serious person can get many of its benefits working alone. Many of the aims of therapy (growth, a sense of cohesion in one's life, and autonomy) can be at least partially achieved on one's own. But special techniques as well as unusual self-discipline and honesty are necessary— even more than in therapy. Therapeutic self-scrutiny does not develop naturally. True, we all look at ourselves and our lives, wondering what's wrong, why things occurred as they did, how to accomplish goals. But this self-searching is generally not therapeutic. We can in fact speak of three stages of introspection, of which only the last is therapeutically valuable.

The first stage is **self-absorption.** One feels at the mercy of outside forces: other people, fate, one's own impulses. There is a tendency to blame others for whatever goes wrong, to feel victimized by circumstances. One feels helpless to change things—and besides, that's the job of those who are creating the problems. One feels engulfed by self-pity, alone, uninvolved with others in the world except as they act for mysterious reasons to create one's destiny.

A more useful stage of self-knowledge is **insightful scrutiny.** One begins to see how one's own behavior and assumptions have an effect on other people: What happens is not due completely to chance or the ill will of the outside world. One has achieved some understanding of the forces—both deep and more superficial—that control one, but one is not yet ready to act to change them. At this stage one has true *insight,* but this is insufficient by itself.

Most valuable is **productive introspection,** which combines insight with responsible action. One knows what can be changed and what cannot and the difference between meaningful and pointless confrontation with the people and situations in one's life. One considers risks and benefits intelligently, but not obsessively, before acting and has a fair idea of the consequences. Good therapy has this as a goal. But it requires effort to maintain this state: It is all too easy, once therapy is terminated, to revert to the earlier stages.

While one can move through these stages without the help of therapy, it is much easier for several reasons to avoid getting stuck at the earlier levels if one is engaged in therapy. First, anxiety is a frequent concomitant of introspection. Problems arise that seem insoluble; fears previously pushed aside now emerge too urgently to be ignored. A therapist provides support during these crises. But when you're facing them by yourself, the pain of what you encounter may make you unable to go on.

A therapist, too, is like a three-way mirror, reflecting sides of the client that are not ordinarily visible. While you can achieve some insight into hidden aspects of yourself on your own, you cannot see yourself from all the perspectives available to a trained and dispassionate person.

Finally, the therapeutic relationship functions as a model of a satisfying real-world relationship, giving the client a glimpse of how people feel and behave responsibly toward each other. In this way, the relationship between therapist and client is a crucial part of learning to learn. While ordinary friendships are somewhat helpful in this process, friends cannot be expected to play the therapist's role.

People who cannot enter therapy can acquire the tools and techniques to create something similar to a productive therapeutic environment. Keeping a **journal** and recording and interpreting one's dreams are two such techniques. For those who have been in therapy previously, these techniques will be more or less familiar and easily relearned. People without previous therapeutic experience have probably had no prior exposure to rigorous techniques for the development of productive introspection. The instructions here are only a very basic guide. The books on journal keeping and dream work suggested at the end of this chapter will be helpful if you feel the need for more guidance.

It is often useful to keep a journal. It is not necessary to make entries in it every day, only during times of crisis. Just the experience of writing about crises can make them less frightening, and focusing on your feelings and reactions will help bring order to them. In this way, a journal performs some of the functions of a therapist.

The form in which you keep journal entries can increase their usefulness. Specificity and clarity are invaluable. So, in writing about a current crisis, note first of all when and how it started and what events precipitated it. Sometimes this isn't apparent—you just find yourself in the middle of something with no clear sense of how you got there. But it is very important to try to trace the crisis back to its origin. There is always a precipitating cause. Identifying it is the first step toward gaining control over your panic. Your aim, in making entries in the journal, is not merely to complain or express emotion, though doing this can make you feel immediately better. If that is all you do, the problem will not be solved, and your distress is apt to return. Your aim is, rather, to achieve enough psychological distance from your panic to enable you to understand it and your role (as well as that of others) in bringing it about, and then to make changes in your attitudes and behavior to insure that it won't happen again.

Next, notice how you are feeling and put your observations into words as precisely and evocatively as you can. You may be tempted to be impressionistic and vague to avoid stirring up even more pain. But only a precise description will give you something concrete to work with. (Remember the discussion of jargon in Chapter 10.) Identify your feelings: Are you scared, sad, angry, lonely? Write at length about that feeling, while you are overwhelmed by it rather than when it has subsided. You do not want a dispassionate account but something that pulsates with emotion and is an accurate picture of your inner world. If you really have very little emotional response to the situation, it can't be a crisis. Think of your journal as a listening therapist; pour out your problems as if to a sympathetic and non-judgmental listener. While you're writing, don't try to make sense of it—don't interpret or edit. You may be tempted, as you write, to make your entry read like a work of literature. But just as when you are talking to a therapist, your job in journal writing is to say whatever comes into your mind without imposing any organization on it. Remember that nobody but you will ever see those pages, so literary quality is unimportant.

Not immediately after you have written, but not more than a few days afterward, look at what you wrote. Try to read what's on the page as an uninvolved person would. Try to pick out important emotional themes: for instance, loss, abandonment, or anger. Now project yourself into those feelings. What are they like? Try to remember times in the past when you have felt the same way. What was going on in your life then? Is there any parallel event or situation now? (The content need not be similar, only the emotional process.) Write your responses to the original entry either on a separate page or in the margin in another color ink. Your comments can be lengthy or as brief as a single word— whatever is needed to make the connection clear, both now and for future rereading.

With this work, you have achieved insight. Your next task is to make changes. Ask yourself what you can do to remedy the present situation as well as to keep the triggering event from occurring again—or to keep it from having the same devastating effect if it does recur. Write this down. Restrict your prescription to changes *you* can make in yourself or your environment, and avoid suggestions that others behave differently toward you. Remember that the only person you can change directly is yourself, though others may change in response to changes they perceive in you.

People often think of change as involving large-scale, dramatic events with obvious external repercussions: marriage, moving, breaking off relationships. But change can be internal and on a smaller scale, yet very powerful. For example, with conscious determination, you can gradually make changes in your behavior—being silent rather than babbling when you're anxious; having sex only when you feel like it, not as a way of pleasing someone; looking people in the eye when talking to them. Isolate the smallest step you can take as the beginning of a larger change and *act on it*. It has been said that a journey of a thousand miles begins with one step, and great changes in life begin with imperceptible alterations in attitude.

Suppose you want to become a completely different kind of person—someone who is (or at least seems) comfortable with other people, self-assured and serene. You can't become that person overnight, even with the best will in the world. Nor can you acquire these attitudes as abstract, indivisible wholes. Rather, each of them is composed of a multitude of smaller attitudes, some externally visible to others, some observable only by introspection. It is useful to remember that imitating an *external* manifestation of an internal state, even when the latter isn't felt, has two important results: Other people assume that your feelings are in accord with your actions and behave toward you as if you actually *were* the self-assured person you are imitating, and you start to feel the emotions and attitudes that go along with the way you're acting—the tail starts to wag the dog. In the same way, your task in keeping your journal is, first, to record, say, your distress at being ill-at-ease at a party, noting what you said and did, and how (exactly) you felt. Then, later, find one particular small thing in this wealth of embarrassments that you can consciously change. Describe the anticipated change in your journal. At the next opportunity, practice it. Note the results.

If the crisis that has inspired your journal entry in fact began with a single and devastating precipitating event, you need to act in response to that event. Suppose you trace your current state of anxiety to a discussion with your husband in which, talking about your friends who are having affairs, he suggested that that wasn't such a bad idea. You were stung: You felt terrified he would leave you, jealous, suspicious. But your immediate response was withdrawal. You changed the subject to something safe. The issue was dropped, but now, the next day or the next week, you feel no better. When you think of that conversation (which you do several times a day), your heart pounds, and you feel dizzy. Withdrawal and denial are inadequate resolutions of such a crisis. You must act directly: In this case, raise the issue again with your husband. It takes courage. While you're not sure how he'll respond, all your mental scenarios are disastrous. But you can't go on in the dark, imagining the worst. You have to be more assertive with him, asking perhaps what he meant by his remark, how seriously he intended it. And if he was serious, how can the two of you reconcile your feelings? By your direct response, you change your state of helpless and diffuse anxiety—perhaps to anger or another negative emotion, but at least to something you can work with. Here, as elsewhere, the mere internal realization on your part of the precipitating cause of your anxiety is not sufficient to make it disappear. You must take action to bring about changes in the real world. *The courage of insight plus the courage of action equals change.*

Here again, once the crisis is over, note in your journal how you handled it, how successful your solution was, and how you feel now. This helps to give you a feeling that the crisis is over and provides a record for next time. The entry serves both as encouragement, showing that you *can* handle crisis and distress, and as guidance, showing the steps to take in the next crisis.

You can continue writing in your journal when there is no crisis, or not; this is up to you. For some people, an ongoing journal is a useful tool for productive introspection. For others, though, insistence on a daily regimen makes it unexciting and dry.

Dream interpretation is another aid to productive introspection. Everyone knows that work on dreams is a fundamental part of insight-oriented psychotherapy, but over the last eighty years, great mysticism has been disseminated about the meaning and use of dreams, so that people are now often both frightened at the power of their dreams and confused about how to make sense of them. Don't worry about that: Just think of your dreams as a useful tool—like the journal, a way to get to know yourself better.

People often worry about not remembering dreams. We know that everyone dreams regularly, about five dreams a night, so it isn't a question of learning to dream but rather of learning to remember the dreams you have. Some theories of psychotherapy assume that failure to remember dreams is indicative of serious problems. But it is just as likely that people forget dreams because they aren't accustomed to remembering them and haven't developed ways of increasing their ability to remember them. If you want to remember dreams and take an interest in them, you will find your recollection getting better and better. There are a few simple, practical steps that make it easier. Keep a pad of paper and a pen with a light in it (available in wilderness-supply and office-supply stores) beside your bed, so that if you wake in the middle of the night with a dream, you won't have to struggle to decide whether to turn on the light or go back to sleep. If you wake up with some pieces of a dream in mind, your first temptation might be to forget them: They're disjointed fragments, apparently meaningless. Or you tell yourself to go back to sleep; you'll remember it in the morning. Both of these assumptions are fallacious and will lead to your forgetting important dream material. (The more dreams you remember, the easier it will be to remember others; it becomes a habit.) If you wake up with a dream, you can jot down a few notes that will jog your memory in the morning: You don't have to get it all down, if that seems too discouraging at 3:00 A.M. Every day, on waking up in the morning, form the habit of asking yourself whether you recall any dreams. If anything comes to mind, no matter how vague or fragmentary, write it down. Do this before you've gotten involved with the business of waking up. Otherwise the fragments will vanish.

When you have a dream, what do you do with it? It is

sometimes assumed that there is a single universal "code" for unraveling the meaning of dream symbols. Flying means sex; a hot dog means sex; eating means sex. But in fact, each person has his/her own unique set of symbols, as well as a unique style of narrative exposition in dreams. After you have examined several of your dreams, you will be able to see patterns emerging that are uniquely meaningful for you. How do you begin to identify these patterns?

1. Write down the whole dream, everything you remember, as clearly as you can.

2. Try to associate to each of the objects, people, and places that occur in the dream: What does each one remind you of? Try to be as specific as possible, remembering all details. Don't discard any associations. For example, a woman who walked past you in your dream looked a little like the teller who gave you cash at the bank earlier that day. You say to yourself: "That's ridiculous. She's totally unimportant to me. She can't be in my dream." But as you think about her, something else in the interaction with the teller strikes you. She was a little abrupt with you as you counted out the money. It reminded you of your mother's impatience with you as a child. An image in a dream often serves a dual function: It stands for something that occurred in your immediate past, called the **day residue** (perhaps something, as here, trivial and hardly noticed), and at the same time, that trivial recent event points like an arrow back to something more significant from long ago. So don't pass over your immediate association because it seems unimportant, but as you start interpreting a dream, think over the events in your day as an opening wedge in the decoding of the dream.

People sometimes worry that dream interpretation is an all-or-nothing activity. If you don't get it right the first time, you'll never have the chance again. (And there is only one "right" answer.) But in fact, the unconscious (where dream symbols originate) is eager to communicate and get its message across. If you don't find a satisfying interpretation the first time, the unconscious will send you the same message in other dreams, using the same or different symbols.

Actually, it is inaccurate to think of dreams as being "about" a single thing, so that a particular interpretation of a dream, or an event in it, is right or wrong. It is said that dream symbols are **"overdetermined"**—a single symbol stands at once for several different things. So you can very easily discover a part of the meaning of a dream without understanding the whole (which may be impossible). But even a part is very useful.

3. Ask yourself: What wish or fear does my dream express (perhaps in a very disguised form)? And don't forget that a "wish" in a dream can be for something that, consciously, you would not want to come true, and likewise, a "fear" can represent something you think you really want. So you may think you wholeheartedly desire to finish your dissertation, but you have a dream in which the manuscript burns. The dream may represent your fear that your work will come to nothing, but it could also suggest that what is keeping you from finishing is an unacknowledged desire not to be done: The dream represents a conscious fear, which itself stands for an unconscious wish. A dream is always an expression of a wish or a fear, even though it may not appear to be.

4. Ask: What is the dream about? What is the theme? This is to be distinguished from the feeling-tone of the dream mentioned below. It is the intellectual content, which can be translated into a sentence or a phrase: "I'm getting older"; "My sexual relationships are a mess"; "I'm always abandoning people." Often what a dream *seems* to be about is not what it is *really* about. This is expressed in psychoanalytic terms as the distinction between the **manifest content** (the surface plot of the dream) and the **latent content** (what the unconscious is attempting to express, usually in disguised form). Your associations to the manifest content lead, bit by bit, to the latent content. You begin to work on a dream by asking what the manifest content reminds you of. Eventually, with this association leading to another deeper association, and so on, you will work your way back to the unconscious meaning the surface symbols have for you— the latent content.

5. Now, try to remember the feeling-tone that accompanied the events in the dream: fear, anger, happiness. The feeling-tone you identify may be appropriate for the dream's thematic content (you dream about success and feel happy), or it may not be (you feel anger or fear at success). If you find a mismatch, assume that the feeling-tone is appropriate for some *part* of you: Perhaps a part of you, of which you are not aware, fears success or is angry because it views the striving to succeed as an unfair burden imposed by a dictatorial parent. Because this feeling is seen by the conscious, rational mind as unacceptable, the only way it can be expressed is through complex and convoluted dream symbolism. Keep in mind that this feeling represents only a part of you—not what you "really want." Do not, in other words, take the messages in dreams as orders that must be acted upon.

Both journal writing and dream interpretation are therapeutically useful in part because they give you distance from your distress. As long as you feel helplessly overwhelmed and caught in the middle of a crisis, or totally at the mercy of your emotions, you cannot work your way out of them. These techniques let you examine yourself from a more rational, external perspective, one that a therapist might take—while at the same time connecting events with their emotional consequences.

The techniques outlined here give you a means of coping with the usual problems of daily life and lessening or avoiding moderate distress. But some symptoms go beyond difficulties in daily life to affect your whole well-being. Concentrating your journal writing and analysis on particular areas can help you understand and mitigate the most common of these, anxiety and depression. (Dreams can be used in the same way.)

The word **anxiety** describes two different emotional states. You may say you are "anxious" when you feel tense and agitated because of a real upcoming event: a party that you are going to give or a visit from your mother. The anxiety connected with these events, while unpleasant, is self-limiting. Once the event has passed, the anxiety will dissipate. Worse is **free-floating anxiety:** a continual state of vague dread and tension with no identifiable external cause. A number of unpleasant physical symptoms can be created by anxiety, among them, heart palpitations, sweaty palms, nausea, diarrhea, and insomnia. Aside from the feelings of fear and suspense directly connected with anxiety, there are other emotional signs of its presence: Especially common are feelings of **depersonalization** (the sense that you are watching yourself speak and act as an uninvolved observer). Particularly frightening is the feeling that this state has descended out of nowhere and will never go away. But if you can discover a triggering event, you are on the way to controlling the anxiety.

In a journal entry, try to recall the moment at which you first began to feel anxious, and remember what was happening at that time. Try to think back to a time when you were free of the feeling, using a specific event in your life to pinpoint that time: "Two weeks ago on Friday when I went to see *Star Wars* with Larry I felt good, but the next night in the Chinese restaurant I couldn't eat. So it must have started between Friday night and Saturday evening." (Referring to an appointment book can be helpful here.) Once you have located the onset of the event in time and recognized the source of the anxiety, you may find yourself feeling even worse and may be tempted to give up. The symptoms of anxiety arise partly to conceal the real source of fear, so that identifying the latter explicitly will at first make you feel worse. But if you persevere, you will find yourself feeling better—freer and more in control. You might feel that your anxiety is so overwhelming and deep that you cannot do anything to dispel it, or that its roots are located too far back in the past to find. But by identifying the current triggering causes, you can begin to eradicate the anxiety.

Begin to work on your anxiety through the following steps:

1. Answer the most important question: *What am I (really) afraid of?* The source may be obvious (your mother's upcoming visit, with her expected continual criticism), or the apparent source of fear (the event you have identified as triggering the anxiety) may prove to be just a substitute for the real one (your mother's visit reminds you that you don't love her, and this in turn reminds you of feeling unloved by her in your childhood).

2. Try to remember a time in the past when you felt the same kind of fear. Was there something similar going on? How did you get over it? Can you use the same method now? Why was the incident so important?

3. Consider your options. How can you remove the source of the anxiety? Can you make changes in the real world—confront the person upsetting you or break off your relationship with that person—or will you have to learn to accept the existing situation (you feel obligated to have your mother visit)? If there is a possibility of change, what is the smallest helpful change you can make in your life? (Since change itself is anxiety-provoking, the smallest change that makes a difference is best.)

4. As you get painfully close to the real basis of the fear, you may be tempted to stop thinking. But you cannot run away from your anxiety. Until you confront it, it will always be there. If you find that your thinking is becoming unproductive, or too much to bear, a break may be helpful: Take a walk, scrub the kitchen floor, work in the garden. Taking a break from the problem may bring you to a solution indirectly. If not, get back to the problem once your mind feels fresher.

The other major debilitating emotion people encounter is **depression.** As with anxiety, it occurs in two forms. One is a response to real events: *e.g.*, death or divorce or the loss of a job. Here you can see the precipitating cause, and after a period of distress, you will normally start to feel better. The other type is more insidious. You often can't tell when it has started or provide a plausible reason for it. And it typically doesn't go away: It may get better or worse, but it becomes a part of your personality. This is the kind of depression for which therapy can be very helpful.

Depression, like anxiety, brings in its train a wide variety of emotional and physical symptoms. People often think of depression as "sadness," but there may be other emotional and physical manifestations: listlessness and fatigue, a lack of interest in anything, impatience and anger. A depressed person may find it difficult to get up in the morning, may sleep a great deal or not at all; may become uninterested in sex or food or may eat compulsively; may get sick more than usual; may ruminate on death, suicide, and the meaninglessness of life.

The steps suggested for coming to grips with anxiety are equally useful for depression, with one change. In the first one, substitute for the question "What am I afraid of?" the question *"What am I sad and/or angry about?"*

Depressions can vary greatly in their seriousness. This advice is most apt to be useful for mild or moderate depressions. If you find, after about a month of trying to put these suggestions into action, that your emotional state has not noticeably improved and the symptoms have not abated, you should seek professional help if at all possible.

Being your own therapist isn't easy, but when it's the only choice, and you follow the guidelines courageously and rigorously, it can be effective. But you must remain vigilant and avoid falling into the trap of self-absorption. These are techniques that you can use all through your life, and like psychotherapy, they can enrich your life and make it more meaningful and rewarding.

SUGGESTED READING

Field, Joanna, *A Life of One's Own.* Boston, Houghton Mifflin, 1981.

Fried, Edrita, *The Courage to Change.* New York, Brunner-Mazel, 1980.

Jones, Richard M., *The New Psychology of Dreams.* New York, Penguin, 1978.

Levenson, Edgar A., *The Fallacy of Understanding.* New York, Basic Books, 1972.

Rainer, Tristine, *The New Diary.* Boston, Houghton Mifflin, 1978.

GLOSSARY

---

adolescent. A person between the ages of thirteen and twenty-five who is financially dependent on his/her parents.

anxiety. A feeling of tension and agitation connected with an upcoming event. **Free-floating anxiety:** A continual state of vague dread and tension with no identifiable external cause.

artist. Someone engaged in creative activity; examples are painters, sculptors, writers, and performers.

autonomy. *See* **power.**

basic trust. The feeling that another person means well toward one and will not do one harm.

brief psychotherapy. Therapy of short duration (less than a year), low intensity (no more than one session per week), usually verbal, with an interpersonal rather than intrapsychic emphasis, and directive.

coercion. Getting people to do things through direct threats of harm.

confidentiality. The ethical principle that requires that the therapist not reveal information gained from a client to anyone else without permission from the client.

control. The restriction of other people's options.

countertransference. A therapist's response to a client based on relationships in the therapist's past. *See* **transference.**

day residue. Material from a dreamer's current life, used in dreams as a basis of their construction.

defenses. Techniques the mind unconsciously makes use of to protect itself from conflict and anxiety—distortions of reality.

dependent person. Someone financially or emotionally dependent on someone else.

depersonalization. The sense that one is watching oneself speak and act as an uninvolved observer.

depression. A combination of emotions and physical sensations that may include: sadness, low spirits, retardation of thought and action, self-hatred, suicidal ideas, and loss of or abnormal appetite, sleep, or sexual desire.

directive vs. non-directive therapy. In **directive therapy,** the therapist tries to influence the client's attitude and behavior by direct suggestion; in **non-directive therapy,** the therapist remains more neutral.

eclectic therapy. A form of therapy in which the therapist borrows techniques from various models, as is appropriate for each client.

established artist. Someone whose work has been given professional and public validation.

extralinguistic communication. Intentional or unintentional expression of ideas and feelings through non-linguistic means, *e.g.*, eye contact, facial expressions, gestures.

fantasy. Imaginary events or mental images.

free association. The mode of thinking encouraged in psychoanalysis involving the following basic rule: to say everything that comes into one's mind without editing or censorship.

hedge. A form of communication that softens the impact of what is being said.

high- (vs. low-) intensity therapy. High-intensity therapy involves more than one session per week; **low-intensity,** one session a week or fewer.

insight. The capacity to understand one's own motives, to be aware of the workings of one's mind, to appreciate the meaning of symbolic behavior.

insightful scrutiny. A level of self-knowledge in which one sees the effects of one's own behavior and attitudes on oneself and others; one sees how one's own behavior, not mere chance or the will of others, has created one's present situation—but one still lacks the capacity to act to create change. *See* **self-absorption** and **productive introspection.**

interpersonal (vs. intrapsychic) therapy. Interpersonal therapy focuses on the client's relations with others in the present; **intrapsychic therapy,** on relations in the client's childhood and how they are currently represented in the client's conscious and unconscious mind.

interpretation. The attribution (by therapist or client) of symbolic meaning to a client's attitudes or behaviors, *e.g.,* dreams, symptoms, or associations. **collaborative interpretation.** Therapist and client working together to create meaningful interpretations, in which each takes responsibility for part of the interpretative structure. **unilateral interpretation.** A therapeutic situation in which the therapist alone is responsible for making all interpretations for the client.

journal. A personal record of one's experiences, not meant for publication.

Jungian analytic psychology. A form of psychotherapy developed by Carl Jung and emphasizing the discovery and interpretation of deeply unconscious symbolic material.

learning to learn. Unconscious process of learning how to learn.

long- (vs. short-) term therapy. Long-term therapy is expected to last more than a year; **short-term,** less than a year.

manifest/latent content (of dreams). Manifest content: The events in a dream as you remember them. **Latent content:** What the dream is really (symbolically) about. This is what dream interpretation reveals.

manipulation. Trying to induce another person to modify behavior by indirect means; not taking responsibility for the attempt.

metacommunication. Communicating about communication.

neurosis. Being stuck in, and unable to break out of, unsatisfactory ways of behaving and feeling that were learned in childhood.

overdetermination. A symptom or a symbol is said to be **overdetermined** if it has more than one meaning; the multiple causality of symptoms or multiple meaning of symbols.

paradox. A situation in which two contradictory ideas are both true.

paralinguistic communication. Oral, but not verbal, communication, consciously intended or not. Speed, loudness, and pitch of articulation are examples.

power. Taking responsibility for what one says, does, and thinks.

productive introspection. The stage of self-knowledge in which one not only understands the reasons for, and consequences of, one's own behavior, but can act to change it. *See* **self-absorption** and **insightful scrutiny.**

psychoanalysis. A form of psychotherapy developed by Sigmund Freud, stressing the interpretation of dreams, associations, and transference.

psychoanalytically oriented psychotherapy. Psychotherapy usually of medium duration and high intensity, and verbal, with an intrapsychic emphasis and a non-directive approach; psychoanalytic in theory but of shorter duration and less intensity.

reciprocity. A relationship in which both participants can do the same thing and their actions will be interpreted and treated in the same way.

referral. Getting the name of a therapist (or other professional).

risk. interpersonal risk. The danger of loss of face or threat of rejection by another person. **intrapsychic risk.** The danger of confronting irrational fears previously hidden. **situational risk.** The danger that a relationship (particularly the therapeutic relationship) is untrustworthy.

self-absorption. That stage of self-knowledge in which one feels at the mercy of outside forces and tends to blame others if things go wrong. *See* **insightful scrutiny** and **productive introspection.**

symbolic gift. A gift that refers to or represents something else, usually indirectly.

transference. The unconscious attribution, by one adult to another, of feelings and attitudes that were characteristic of important people earlier in life. *See* **countertransference.**

verbal ("talking") therapy vs. non-verbal therapy. Verbal therapy is done mostly through linguistic communication—the client talks, the therapist speaks in response. **Non-verbal therapy** may refer to either of two situations: The client's non-verbal communication is the focus of therapeutic work, or the therapist's interventions are non-verbal, involving, *e.g.*, drugs or electric shock. *See* **extralinguistic communication.**

YAVIS. An acronym for the type of clients therapists prefer to work with, and who consequently enter therapy more often and stay in it longer: Young, Attractive, Verbal, Intelligent, and Successful.

INDEX